"Soong-Chan Rah adds a significant voice to the rich and growing interpretive corpus on the book of Lamentations. He brings to his study a special attentiveness to the rootage of lament in Korean religious tradition. As Western culture is increasingly in 'free fall,' there is compelling reason to pay steady attentiveness to Lamentations. Rah's book will be of great value in that now-required attentiveness."

Walter Brueggemann, Columbia Theological Seminary

"In the hands of Soong-Chan Rah, the book of Lamentations becomes a provocative and prophetic call for justice and solidarity with the voiceless, oppressed and suffering in our cities. *Prophetic Lament* is a treasure-trove of biblical truth, historical understanding, theological insight, and contemporary application and relevance. More than a biblical commentary, *Prophetic Lament* is needed medicine for a Christianity enamored with a *theologia gloriae* and not the wisdom and power of a *theologia crucis*. This is a book to read, ponder and live out."

Eldin Villafañe, professor of Christian social ethics, Gordon-Conwell Theological Seminary

"As a product of the African-American and urban church I am grateful for this important resource on the mission of God in the context of suffering. Soong-Chan Rah's transparent, prophetic and practical voice comes through in powerful and deeply insightful ways on the pages. In a time when too many churches are held captive to a feel-good and happy-rich gospel, this book shows us a more authentic biblical narrative."

Efrem Smith, president and CEO, World Impact

"Through the lamentations of a people who lost their way and finally found their voice, Rah penetrates our false narratives and selective memory. He exposes the racial story of a deaf, dumb and blind US church, bearing the image of lifeless idols that have rested precariously on the sands of false identity and entitlement. With compassion and razor-sharp precision, Rah teaches us, wide-eyed or wincing, to sing these hope-filled songs of lament. In the process, we begin to see, hear and speak faithfully to and with a compassionate God whose Son, well acquainted with grief and lament, still bears our human image and sings for and with us as king and high priest."

Cherith Nordling, associate professor of theology, Northern Seminary

"Finally, a book that rightly commends lament as the best way to interpret and reckon with the pain and suffering so prominent in today's news! The book also gives Lamentations, an oft-overlooked biblical book, a voice—a very fresh voice—in that reckoning. The author's scholarship is first-rate, his style winsome and true to life, and his message occasionally hard hitting but always hugely relevant. An important book for openhearted evangelicals."

Bob Hubbard, North Park Theological Seminary

"I recommend this book to anyone who wishes to understand and embrace a fuller, more authentic and more just expression of Christianity. *Prophetic Lament* is more evidence of Soong-Chan Rah becoming one of the most important theologians of our time, and one of the few who truly understand the world into which theology must now enter."

Jim Wallis, author of *The UnCommon Good*, president of Sojourners

"*Prophetic Lament* teaches readers about one of the most critical and appropriate responses to suffering in this world. The integration of spiritual lament and a prophetic call for justice is a critical reminder for the contemporary church to return to the truths of Scripture as we seek to understand tragedy and brokenness. Soong-Chan Rah powerfully reminds readers that an evangelical theology devoid of lament lacks the foundational depth of one of the most significant spiritual practices of the people of God. This book provocatively challenges the church to embody a 'full narrative of Christ in his suffering and in his triumph.'"

Mae Elise Cannon, author of *Social Justice Handbook* and *Just Spirituality*

"Soong-Chan Rah challenges the notion of American evangelicalism rooted in arrogant triumphalism and lifeless consumerism. He calls us to lament, to truly engage in the suffering of our neighbors and thus experience the great hope of God. *Prophetic Lament* has tremendous insight and profound ministry implications for church planters, urban ministers and all who follow Jesus as he loves and disciples sinners in this broken world."

John Teter, senior pastor, Fountain of Life Covenant Church

"*Prophetic Lament* weaves a compelling analysis of the book of Lamentations with American theological history and the economic and racial justice crisis we face today in the United States. As the American church seeks to find our prophetic voice, Dr. Rah reminds us the best place to start is with deep tones of lament."

Troy Jackson, director, AMOS Project, coauthor of *Forgive Us*

"This book illuminates the resilient faith of a current lamenter's raw trust in God. Everyone engaged in the shared struggle to hope in the midst of a violent and unjust world ought to read this accessible integration of biblical text, witness and sharp insight into the present cultural realties of the American church. Readers will discover a pithy prophetic response to the reality of shame, the problem of privilege and the possibilities of honor, hope and worship with integrity. This volume is a credit to the Resonate series."

James K. Bruckner, North Park Theological Seminary

PROPHETIC LAMENT

A Call for Justice in Troubled Times

Soong-Chan Rah

FOREWORD BY
Brenda Salter McNeil

IVP Books

An imprint of InterVarsity Press
Downers Grove, Illinois

InterVarsity Press
P.O. Box 1400,
Downers Grove, IL 60515-1426
ivpress.com
email@ivpress.com

InterVarsity Press® is the book-publishing division of InterVarsity Christian Fellowship/USA®, a movement of students and faculty active on campus at hundreds of universities, colleges and schools of nursing in the United States of America, and a member movement of the International Fellowship of Evangelical Students. For information about local and regional activities, visit intervarsity.org.

All Scripture quotations, unless otherwise indicated, are taken from THE HOLY BIBLE, NEW INTERNATIONAL VERSION®, NIV® Copyright © 1973, 1978, 1984, 2011 by Biblica, Inc.™ Used by permission. All rights reserved worldwide.

While any stories in this book are true, some names and identifying information may have been changed to protect the privacy of individuals.

Material taken and adapted from "The Necessity of Lament for Ministry in the Urban Context" that appeared in Ex Auditu vol. 29, 2013, is used by permission from Wipf and Stock Publishers.

Cover design: Cindy Kiple
Interior design: Beth McGill
Images: Couple Reaching Up by Evelyn Williams, Private Collection, Bridgeman Images

ISBN 978-0-8308-3694-9 (print)
ISBN 978-0-8308-9761-2 (digital)

Printed in the United States of America ♾

Library of Congress Cataloging-in-Publication Data
Rah, Soong-Chan.
  Prophetic lament : a call for justice in troubled times / Soong-Chan Rah.
    pages cm. -- (Resonate series)
  Includes bibliographical references.
  ISBN 978-0-8308-3694-9 (pbk. : alk. paper)
  1. Bible. Lamentations--Commentaries. I. Title.
  BS1535.53.R34 2015
  224'.307--dc23
                                                                                    2015022730

P 20 19 18 17 16 15 14 13 12 11 10 9 8 7 6 5 4 3 2 1

Y 32 31 30 29 28 27 26 25 24 23 22 21 20 19 18 17 16 15

This book is dedicated to three of the most important

influences in my life:

My mother, Im Hee Rah, my example.

My wife, Sue Rah, my strength.

My daughter, Annah Rah, my hope.

Three generations of female voices that have shaped my voice.

CONTENTS

FOREWORD

by Brenda Salter McNeil

The church has lost its ability to lament!" This heartfelt cry came
from a seminary student as she prayed with other graduate students,
faculty and staff who gathered together to seek God for racial justice
and reconciliation throughout our nation. As we cried and prayed together we realized that our theology and spiritual formation hadn't
given us sufficient permission, language or tools to adequately sit with
the despair and sadness of recent racial injustices, senseless acts of gun
violence and social unrest taking place in the world around us. We even
saw this on social media where people also seemed paralyzed and
helpless to know what to do and how to respond. Sincere, well-meaning
Christian people asked, "What should we do?" while people who were
fed up with the seeming indifference of those around them expressed
their outrage through a hashtag that proclaimed "Silence is Violence!"

All of this reminded me of when my brother and friend, Soong-
Chan Rah, asked me to write the foreword to this book. His request
came when we were both in Ferguson, Missouri, with thirty to forty
other evangelical leaders for a faith roundtable to strategize how
the Christian church should respond to the social unrest and the

rising civil rights movement emerging after the shooting death of an unarmed black teenager by a white police officer. We gathered together to learn and to envision the ways that we might guide the church and the country in the process of healing and reconciliation. On the last day of our gathering we received the shockingly disturbing news that police officers who strangled and killed an African American man on video, while he repeatedly cried, "I can't breathe!" would not be indicted. One young black man in our meeting took this news exceptionally hard and had to be taken out of the room as he wept aloud. One of the elder stateswomen in the group quickly called for us to sing a song of lament. In response, a black female worship leader began to lead us in an upbeat chorus about "taking back what the devil had stolen from us and placing him under our feet!" As I stood near a black male colleague from another theological seminary, we held hands and remained silent. Then he leaned down and whispered in my ear in a concerned voice, "I feel very uncomfortable with this. What does this have to do with lament?!" Of course, he was right. Even though many of us had been nurtured in the rich tradition of the African American church that taught us to sing songs like "Nobody Knows the Trouble I've Seen," "I Must Tell Jesus," "Precious Lord, Take My Hand" and "Sometimes I Feel Like a Motherless Child," somehow we had also lost our historic and spiritual legacy of being able to corporately lament.

It is situations like these that remind me of why all of us desperately need this strategic and prophetic book. From start to finish it offers us the theological tools and practical insights to develop a prophetic imagination that envisions and advocates for the world as God intended it to be. In my opinion, there is no one who is better equipped to help us engage in this important work than Soong-Chan Rah. I have worked with, served alongside and learned from his wise and academically rich teaching on numerous occasions. In all these capacities he is profoundly brilliant, intellectually insightful, spiritually inspiring and socially relevant.

Dr. Rah is one of the leading evangelical voices in the world today. He is also humbly and consistently living out the values he espouses in his personal life with his family and friends and through his professional pursuits. He embodies the type of leadership I call emerging Christian reconcilers to emulate as I speak and consult about the issue of racial reconciliation around the world. Soong-Chan Rah knows that these emerging leaders are just like the young woman in our prayer meeting crying out to God for new language and skills to lament the complex social justice issues that they face. This book is an answer to that prayer and offers all of us a better way forward.

Series Introduction

We live in an increasingly biblically illiterate culture—not simply in terms of knowing what the Bible says but also in knowing how God wants to use his Word to draw us closer to him. The contemporary situation has drawn greater attention to the need for biblical and theological reflection that is culturally engaging. Yet the need isn't new.

In every age and in every region of the world, the church needs to be concerned for the biblical sense (what does this particular book of the Bible mean?) and its cultural significance (what does it have to say to us in our particular setting?), never confusing the two but always relating them. Only then can our reflections resonate well both with Scripture *and* with people's life situations. As you can imagine, it's a daunting challenge.

This is the challenge I face daily in my work as a professor at Multnomah Biblical Seminary in Portland, Oregon, and as director of its Institute for the Theology of Culture: New Wine, New Wineskins (new-wineskins.org). Many of my students do not come from Christian homes and have never been exposed to Scripture in a meaningful way, but they often come well-equipped to engage pop culture. Other students have been long entrenched in the Christian subculture and struggle to engage meaningfully in a pluralistic context that does not recognize the Bible as truthful and authoritative for life. Thankfully, Portland is a wonderful living laboratory in which to prepare for ministry within an increasingly diverse setting—ministry that brings the Bible to bear on that context in a theologically sound and grace-filled manner.

The aim of the Resonate series is to provide spiritual nourishment that is biblically sound, theologically orthodox and culturally significant. The form each volume in the series will take is that of an extended essay—each author writing about a biblical book in an interactive, reflective and culturally engaging manner.

Why this approach? There are scores of commentaries on the market from biblical scholars who go verse by verse through the biblical text. While these works are extremely important, there is an increasingly urgent need for pastors who feel at home in the biblical text to bring that text home to today's Christ-followers. They do this by interacting with the text expositionally, placing it within the context of contemporary daily life and viewing their personal stories in light of the original context and unfolding drama of ancient Scripture. There is also a need for people who feel at home in contemporary culture but who are foreigners to Scripture to inhabit the world of the Bible without abandoning their own context. God would have us live in both worlds.

Speaking of context, it is worth noting how this series emerged. I was participating at a consultation on the future of theological inquiry at the Center of Theological Inquiry in Princeton, New Jersey, when David Sanford (former managing editor of the series) contacted me to ask if I would serve as executive editor for Resonate. His timing could not have been better. During the consultation in Princeton, we discussed the need for academics to be more intentional about writing to popular culture and not focus exclusively on writing to our peers in the scholarly guild. We also discussed how greater efforts needed to be made to bridge the academy and the church.

In addition to dialoguing with David Sanford and sketching out what I would envision for such a series, I spoke with several biblical scholars during the consultation. One went so far as to tell me there was no need for another commentary series, for there was an overabundance of them on the market. But when they heard the vision for Resonate, they encouraged me to move forward with it. Like them, I believe a series of this kind could go a long way toward encouraging and equipping today's pastors and teachers to engage each book of the Bible in a thoughtful and rigorous manner.

Some volumes in this series are written by thoughtful practitioners and others by practically oriented academics. Whether practitioner or academic, each author approaches the subject matter not from the standpoint of detached observer but rather as a fully engaged participant in the text—always working with the community of editors I have assembled for the series along with the editorial team at InterVarsity Press.

Instead of proceeding verse by verse, the author of each Resonate volume draws insights from the featured book's major themes, all the while attentive to the context in which these themes are developed. The authors' purposes are to guide, guard and grow readers as they move forward in their own spiritual journeys. In addition to focusing on the major themes of the book under consideration, each author also locates that particular book within the context of the triune God's overarching narrative of holy love for Israel, church and world.

Our aim with this distinctive new genre is to have one finger in the ancient Scriptures, another in the daily newspaper and another touching the heart, all the while pointing to Jesus Christ. This is no easy task, of course, but when accomplished it is extremely rewarding.

Each contributor to Resonate seeks to bear witness to Jesus Christ, the living Word of God, through the written Word in and through his or her own life story and the broader cultural context. So often we go around Scripture to Jesus or we stop short at Scripture and fail to penetrate it to get to Jesus' heart—which is the Father's heart too. Instead, each of us needs to depend on God's Spirit to discern how our culturally situated words and stories are included in the biblical metanarrative, and to learn how to bring God's Word home to our hearts and lives in a truthful and meaningful manner.

We trust that you will find this and other Resonate volumes beneficial as you exegete Scripture and culture in service to Jesus Christ, church and world, and as God exegetes your heart through his Word and Spirit. With this in mind, we dedicate this series as a whole to you as you embark on this arduous and incredible journey.

Paul Louis Metzger, PhD
Executive Editor, Resonate

THE RESONATE
EDITORIAL TEAM

EXECUTIVE EDITOR

Paul Louis Metzger, PhD, professor of Christian theology and theology of culture, Multnomah Biblical Seminary; director, Institute for the Theology of Culture: New Wine, New Wineskins, Multnomah University

MANAGING EDITORS

Beyth Hogue Greenetz and Samantha Black, administrative coordinators, Institute for the Theology of Culture: New Wine, New Wineskins, Multnomah University

OLD TESTAMENT CONSULTING EDITORS

Karl Kutz, PhD, professor of Bible and biblical languages, Multnomah University, and Daniel Somboonsiri, MDiv, theological studies, teaching fellow, Multnomah Biblical Seminary/Multnomah University, fellow, Green Scholar's Initiative

NEW TESTAMENT CONSULTING EDITOR

Albert H. Baylis, PhD, professor of Bible and theology, Multnomah Biblical Seminary/Multnomah University

ivpress.com/resonate

Introduction

A Call to Lament

In the summer of 1996, my wife and I led a church-planting effort in inner-city Cambridge, Massachusetts. Cambridge, which twins the larger sister city of Boston, hosts two world-class universities: Harvard University and the Massachusetts Institute of Technology. Central Square, the neighborhood sandwiched between Harvard and MIT, serves as the locus of civic life in Cambridge. The university students refer to Central Square as "Central Scare." It is the scary urban neighborhood into which you dare not venture, but our church deliberately chose this location. We planted our church with the hope of launching outreach to our inner-city neighborhood and fostering an intentionally multiethnic church community.

The church initially drew its membership from the colleges and universities in close proximity to the church. The students that came to our church were recipients of educational opportunities unavailable to most of the world's population. Members were attracted to the urban vision of the church but were not necessarily city-raised or city-wise individuals. Many were coming to the church to learn about urban ministry and life in the city, so while the urban vision of the church was an attraction, most of the church members had little to no roots in the city. Part of our church vision reflected the desire to motivate young, educated individuals to connect with the city and find ways to engage in urban ministry. Our newly formed community struggled with the central question of how an affluent and privileged community would intersect with the poor in the "Central Scare" neighborhood.

As we geared up to conduct our first public service in September, I grappled with which sermon series would be an appropriate introduction to this fledgling church. The Gospel of Mark seemed like a natural choice since the story of Jesus should be the center of the Christian community. Maybe a nice Pauline letter like Romans would provide the opportunity to teach a systematic, theological structure for a young congregation. I even considered preaching on the book of Revelation and the story of God's plan for the heavenly city.

But after the requisite, initial round of opening services, my first full sermon series for the new church plant was a six-week exposition on the book of Lamentations, a seemingly illogical choice being both from the Old Testament and a downer of a book. It was not a typical sermon series for a new church plant. Church growth books would not advocate for six weeks of lamenting as a way to spark interest in a new church. There's not a whole lot of "user friendliness" or "seeker sensitivity" in what some consider a rather depressing book in the biblical canon.

Years later I recognized God's providence in directing me toward Lamentations. The triumph-and-success orientation of our typical church member needed the corrective brought by stories of struggle and suffering. These stories should not merely provide a sprinkling of flavor for the existing triumphalistic narrative that furthers the privilege of those in the dominant culture. The tendency to view the holistic work of the church as the action of the privileged toward the marginalized often derails the work of true community healing.

Ministry in the urban context, acts of justice and racial reconciliation require a deeper engagement with the other—an engagement
that acknowledges suffering rather than glossing over it.

Theologian Randy Woodley identifies this deeper engagement as
the Hebrew word *shalom*, which is often translated simplistically as
"peace." Woodley asserts that shalom "is active and engaged, going far
beyond the mere absence of conflict. A fuller understanding of shalom
is the key to the door that can lead us to a whole new way of living in
the world."[1] Shalom combats the dualism rampant in Western culture
and is instead rooted in a more Hebraic "passion for equilibrium, a
sense of system in which all the parts cohere."[2] Shalom, therefore,
does not eschew or diminish the role of the other or the reality of a
suffering world. Instead, it embraces the suffering other as an instru-
mental aspect of well-being. Shalom requires lament.

The Old Testament is composed of many different genres, including poetry. Within the genre of poetry exists many subgenres.
Old Testament scholar Claus Westermann situates the Hebrew poetic
material into two broad categories: praise and lament. Westermann
asserts that "as the two poles, they determine the nature of all speaking
to God."[3] Psalms that express worship for the good things that God
has done are categorized as praise hymns. Laments are prayers of
petition arising out of need. But lament is not simply the presentation
of a list of complaints, nor merely the expression of sadness over difficult circumstances. Lament in the Bible is a liturgical response to the
reality of suffering and engages God in the context of pain and trouble.
The hope of lament is that God would respond to human suffering
that is wholeheartedly communicated through lament.

Unfortunately, lament is often missing from the narrative of the
American church. In *Journey Through the Psalms*, Denise Hopkins
examines the use of lament in the major liturgical denominations
in America. The study found that in the *Lutheran Book of Worship*,
the Episcopalian *Book of Common Prayer*, the Catholic *Lectionary*

for Mass, the *Hymnal of the United Church of Christ* and the *United Methodist Hymnal*, "the majority of Psalms omitted from liturgical use are the laments."[4]

This trend is found not only in the mainline traditions but in less liturgical traditions as well. In *Hurting with God*, Glenn Pemberton notes that lament constitutes 40 percent of all psalms, but only 13 percent of the hymnal for the Churches of Christ, 19 percent of the Presbyterian hymnal and 13 percent of the Baptist hymnal.[5] Christian Copyright Licensing International (CCLI) licenses local churches in the use of contemporary worship songs and tracks the songs that are most frequently sung in local churches. CCLI's list of the top one hundred worship songs in August of 2012 reveals that only five of the songs would qualify as a lament. Most of the songs reflect themes of praise: "How Great Is Our God," "Here I Am to Worship," "Happy Day," "Indescribable," "Friend of God," "Glorious Day," "Marvelous Light" and "Victory in Jesus."

The American church avoids lament. The power of lament is minimized and the underlying narrative of suffering that requires lament is lost. But absence doesn't make the heart grow fonder. Absence makes the heart forget. The absence of lament in the liturgy of the American church results in the loss of memory. We forget the necessity of lamenting over suffering and pain. We forget the reality of suffering and pain.

In his book *Peace*, Walter Brueggemann writes about this contrast between a theology of the "have-nots" versus a theology of the "haves." The "have-nots" develop a theology of suffering and survival. The "haves" develop a theology of celebration. Those who live under suffering live "their lives aware of the acute precariousness of their situation." Worship that arises out of suffering cries out for deliverance. "Their notion of themselves is that of a dependent people crying out for a vision of survival and salvation." Lament is the language of suffering.[6]

Those who live in celebration "are concerned with questions of *proper management and joyous celebration.*" Instead of deliverance, they seek constancy and sustainability. "The well-off do not expect their faith to begin in a cry, but rather, in a song. They do not expect or need intrusion, but they rejoice in stability [and the] durability of a world and social order that have been beneficial to them." Praise is the language of celebration.[7]

Christian communities arising from celebration do not want their lives changed, because their lives are in a good place. Tax rates should remain low. Home prices and stocks should continue to rise unabated, while interest rates should remain low to borrow more money to feed a lifestyle to which they have become accustomed.

Lament recognizes the struggles of life and cries out for justice against existing injustices. The status quo is not to be celebrated but instead must be challenged. If tax rates favor the rich, they should be challenged. Redistribution of wealth would not be a catastrophe but instead a blessing in contrast to the existing state of economic inequality. The balance in Scripture between praise and lament is lost in the ethos and worldview of American evangelical Christianity with its dominant language of praise. Any theological reflection that emerges from the suffering "have-nots" can be minimized in the onslaught of the triumphalism of the "haves."

What do we lose as a result of this imbalance? American Christians that flourish under the existing system seek to maintain the existing dynamics of inequality and remain in the theology of celebration over and against the theology of suffering. Promoting one perspective over the other, however, diminishes our theological discourse. To only have a theology of celebration at the cost of the theology of suffering is incomplete. The intersection of the two threads provides the opportunity to engage in the fullness of the gospel message. Lament and praise must go hand in hand.

Walter Brueggemann asks the question:

What happens when appreciation of the lament as a form of speech and faith is lost, as I think it is largely lost in contemporary usage? What happens when the speech forms that redress power distribution have been silenced and eliminated? The answer, I believe, is that a theological monopoly is reinforced, docility and submissiveness are engendered, and the outcome in terms of social practice is to reinforce and consolidate the political-economic monopoly of the status quo.[8]

For American evangelicals riding the fumes of a previous generation's assumptions, a triumphalistic theology of celebration and privilege rooted in a praise-only narrative is perpetuated by the absence of lament and the underlying narrative of suffering that informs lament.

The loss of lament in the American church reflects a serious theological deficiency. This work attempts to remedy that imbalance by providing commentary on a neglected book of the Bible. The suffering endured by God's people resulting from the fall of Jerusalem provides the backdrop for the poetic struggle offered in Lamentations. Lamentations provides the biblical text and the theological lens through which we examine the themes of urban ministry, justice and racial reconciliation. We will seek to find contemporary application of the book of Lamentations within these current themes.

Lamentations responds to the destruction of Jerusalem and the temple in 586 B.C.[9] This collection of poetic reflections emerges from the rubble of a Jerusalem laid waste by the Babylonians. A multitude of voices are raised by the survivors of the devastation and are brought together in a coherent, unified corporate lament. In all likelihood, these laments offered by the remnant in Jerusalem were presented in a unified form by one of the few learned survivors of the Babylonian conquest, the prophet Jeremiah, who is attributed authorship of Lamentations in early church tradition. In five chapters, five related but self-contained accounts tell the story of the aftermath of the fall of Jerusalem.

In Lamentations 1, we explore the shame of suffering and lament in the context of death. The city of Jerusalem has died, so the first chapter of Lamentations reminds us of the deep pain experienced by the community as a result of this death. How we deal with the reality of shame and death often reveals our relationship with others who suffer. Next we examine how Lamentations 2 seeks to understand the source of suffering. How we respond to the possibility of God's sovereignty in the midst of suffering reveals our ability to engage in the depth of lament. We also deal with our role as privileged celebrants when we encounter the suffering other. Lamentations 3 reflects on our engagement with the full expression of human suffering, calls us to examine our worship life and seeks a form of spiritual expression that honors those that suffer. Lamentations 4 reminds us that God deserves all of our respect while our human achievements merit none of his respect. It reveals how the lament that we offer should reflect our understanding of God at work, even in the midst of suffering. Finally, we examine Lamentations 5 as it calls us to join in a corporate lament prayer. This corporate lament offers the hope that God will provide the answers even if the answers are not self-evident.

The ancient book of Lamentations is not a familiar book to many American Christians. At several points in this commentary, I will offer insight from the genre of lament and the historical context that shed light on the text of Lamentations. While some material may be a review for the reader, visiting the literary and historical context is necessary to the exegesis of the text. Toward that end, some material that may be deemed introductory will be found throughout the body of the text.

Despite its age, Lamentations offers us a prophetic critique of what passes for gospel witness in our time. This critique offers fresh insight into our ecclesiology, or more precisely, how the North

American Christian community should respond to a broken world. The major themes—the importance of lament, the necessity of engaging with suffering, the power of encountering the other—should lead us to a theology of lament that corrects the triumphalism of Christianity in the West. Lamentations may serve as the prophetic corrective necessary to embrace the next phase of Christianity.

Lamentations 1

I t is a moment very few people forget—the moment your father dies. For most of my life, I had a tumultuous relationship with my father. He abandoned our family when I was young and, understandably, I resented his absence. His departure left us in dire financial straits, and we ended up living in a low-income, inner-city neighborhood in Baltimore. My mom took two low-paying jobs to keep our family together, but her long work hours resulted in *both* my parents being out of the home. Deep-seated animosity built up over the years toward my father. Infrequent and irregular contact with him only fueled my resentment and anger.

Then in his seventies, my dad returned home. Nearly destitute, he took advantage of the graciousness of my mom, who received him back home. She declared that it was the responsibility of the mature Christians (the rest of the family) to extend grace to the one who had wandered away from the faith. She embodied the story of the gracious father loving the prodigal son.

Not long after my father returned to my mom's house, he suffered a major stroke. After several weeks in the hospital the prognosis was not good, and he was moved from the hospital to hospice where he would linger for nearly a month. My wife, newborn daughter and I were living in Massachusetts when my father was incapacitated in Maryland, so I flew down right after the first stroke. That trip resulted in aggravating my animus toward my father. Not only had he returned after years away, but also he had returned just in time to saddle my mom with the medical bills and to further burden his family. I went back to Massachusetts but returned several weeks later when I was told that he might not have long to live. By this point, my anger had amplified along with his mounting medical bills. I went to his bedside but did not give thought to the reality of his imminent death.

Later that evening I found myself in the family waiting room listening to my mom and my sisters as they began to talk in detail about the funeral arrangements, an event that would happen in just a few more days. It finally hit me with full force that my dad was really going to die. I left the waiting room, rushed over to my father's room and kicked out my nieces and nephews. Alone with my dad, I sat by his bed and clasped his hand in mine. Through tears and with a tight grip on his hand, I offered him my complete forgiveness. I asked for his forgiveness for the years of bitterness I had harbored against him. Through his tears and his tightening grip, we were reconciled just hours before his death.

The reconciliation that occurred with my father on his deathbed required an important realization on my part: my father was dying and this could be my last chance to talk to him. Our history—a history of loss and pain—took on added meaning when I acknowledged the reality of his death. That reality changed the equation.

Everything dies eventually. The best and worst of lives come to an earthly end. Kingdoms and empires wax and wane. Cities have their moments in the sun then fall into disrepair only to rise up surprisingly from the ashes. Different eras of the church come and go. Local churches are planted and churches shut down. Even churches with impressive buildings made of crystal can declare bankruptcy. Death and its impact cannot be avoided; it must be dealt with. The reality of death and the ongoing cycle of life and death remind us that through it all, YHWH[1] remains Lord over all. The question is not whether there will be death, but how we will understand and address this reality.

In Lamentations 1, we encounter a people who have experienced a great loss. Jerusalem has died, and the reality of this tragic event elicits lament. As the people of God recount their suffering and their painful history, they call out to God in the midst of their shame and ask many of the same questions we ask today: Where is our hope even in the midst of suffering and death? Can we see God in all circumstances of life? Does our understanding of a historical reality impact our current reality? Does our response to God reflect our understanding of a shameful history and a painful story that must be acknowledged in the face of death?

THE REALITY OF SUFFERING AND DEATH

The Historical Context of Lamentations

Lamentations does not occur in a vacuum. Historical circumstances shape the unique and specific responses that emerge. The devastating effects of the destruction of Jerusalem in 586 B.C. serve as the context and impetus for the poetry of Lamentations. Not only does Lamentations address a specific moment in Jewish history, but it also addresses a disaster of catastrophic proportions for God's people.

Lamentations 1:1-3 offers an overview of Jerusalem's fall. Verse 1 begins with a description of Jerusalem, "who once was great among the nations," "once so full of people," and "queen among the provinces." The once great and prominent status of Jerusalem contrasts with her current state. She is now "a slave," "a widow" and "deserted." In verse 2 we are introduced to her emotions as "bitterly she weeps at night, tears are on her cheeks." Verse 3 summarizes her experience as "affliction and harsh labor." The background story that leads to Lamentations culminates with the exile in verse 3: "Judah has gone into exile. She dwells among the nations; she finds no resting place."

(It is noteworthy that Jerusalem is personified as a female. A later section will explore the significance of this personification.) Jerusalem finds herself alone with no one to turn to for help. The city of Jerusalem has moved from being the capital of a great nation to isolation and alienation, with many of her residents sent away into exile. Delbert Hillers notes that the opening cry of Lamentations 1:1 has the effect of "an incredulous question: 'How can it be that . . . ?'— an expression of the speaker's astonishment, grief or indignation at what has happened."[1] The first three verses of Lamentations remind the community why lament is necessary: a national tragedy has occurred. In verses 1 and 2, Adele Berlin finds that "the division into two groups of lines corresponds to the two parallel comparisons between Jerusalem's past and her present."[2] Lamentations 1:1-2 presents the contrast between the Jerusalem of a previous era and its current state. This reality rooted in a historical event provides the setting for the lament that follows. The fall of a once-great city provides the background for the emotional depth in Lamentations.

The big picture context for the book of Lamentations emerges from God's historical relationship to the children of Israel. Under the reigns of David and Solomon, the nation of Israel flourished. After King Solomon's death, two kingdoms emerged: the northern kingdom of Israel and the southern kingdom of Judah. Ultimately, both kingdoms were exiled as punishment for their infidelity and unfaithfulness to their covenant with YHWH, with the fall of the northern kingdom preceding the fall of the southern kingdom of Judah. Jerusalem as the capital of Judah was the final holdout against conquerors from the north, and a long siege ended in its eventual conquest by the Babylonian marauders.

The fall of Jerusalem to the Babylonians meant complete devastation to the city and her residents. The Babylonians were ruthless conquerors who followed a scorched-earth policy, burning and salting the fields so subsequent crops would be compromised, then proceeding to fill the wells. They destroyed the nation and the land. Particularly upset that Jerusalem had resisted, the Babylonians showed no mercy. As historian John Bright describes: "The land had been completely wrecked. Its cities destroyed, its economy ruined, its leading citizens killed or deported, the population consisted chiefly of poor peasants considered incapable of making trouble."[3] The remnant of Jerusalem stood in utter dismay at the destruction of their once-great city. Jerusalem had measured herself through worldly standards of wealth and prosperity. Now that Jerusalem lay in ruins, those standards were out of reach.

The destruction of Jerusalem serves as the apex of suffering for God's people. The last stronghold for a formerly great nation fell, inaugurating the exilic period for God's people. When this tragedy occurs, the people of God tumble to the depth of despair. In Jeremiah 29, we are given a glimpse of two possible responses to the national tragedy of exile. On the one hand, God's people were tempted to withdraw from the world. On the other, they were tempted to return to their idolatrous ways. Lamentations 1:1-3 reminds us of the tragic set of circumstances that confronts God's people. They have fallen from the heights. A vibrant city filled with people now lies deserted. A noble queen has now become a slave (v. 1). How will the people of God respond to this tragedy?

Although the proper response to the historical reality of this text is the lament offered in Lamentations, Jeremiah 29 presents two unacceptable options available to God's people sent away into exile. Jeremiah responds to the situation described in Lamentations 1:1-3 by sending a letter "from Jerusalem to the surviving elders among the exiles and to the priests, the prophets and all the other people Nebuchadnezzar had carried into exile from Jerusalem to Babylon" (Jer 29:1). Jeremiah 29:4-7 reveals YHWH's command for the exiles when they are tempted to withdraw from the world:

This is what the LORD Almighty, the God of Israel, says to all
those I carried into exile from Jerusalem to Babylon: "Build
houses and settle down; plant gardens and eat what they
produce. Marry and have sons and daughters; find wives for
your sons and give your daughters in marriage, so that they
too may have sons and daughters. Increase in number there;
do not decrease. Also, seek the peace and prosperity of the
city to which I have carried you into exile. Pray to the LORD
for it, because if it prospers, you too will prosper."

The call in Psalms to seek the peace and prosperity of Jerusalem
is turned on its head with the command in Jeremiah 29:7 to "seek
the peace and prosperity of the city to which I have carried you into
exile," that is, Babylon. The familiar formula and the anticipated call
to seek the peace of Jerusalem would have been a sign of hope that
the exiles could turn their attention back to the Promised Land.
Instead, they are commanded (very unexpectedly) to seek the
shalom of Babylon. YHWH implores his people to continue to live
life, even in the midst of shattered dreams and expectations. They
are to conduct life in all its fullness, including building homes,
planting gardens, getting married and increasing in number. Even
in the midst of a foreign land, they are not to hide from the world,
but instead seek ways to engage and even contribute. Life continues
even as a community struggles with its place and identity. Escape
from the reality of a fallen world is not an option. Jeremiah confronts the desire by a defeated people to give up and run away. The
reality of Lamentations 1:1-3 should not result in the impulse to
escape, but instead should result in engagement.

The exiles were disheartened by how far they had fallen as evidenced by Lamentations 1:1-3. God's people were tempted to flee
and disengage from the world around them in response to their
reality, but Jeremiah 29:4-7 challenges God's people to not take that

option. Jeremiah's letter to the exiles does not allow for that option. The people of God are to seek the peace of Babylon and not to disengage with the ready-made excuse that Babylon is a wicked city. They are not to give in to the temptation to withdraw from the world when things are not going as they had planned.

JERUSALEM AND AMERICAN CHRISTIANITY

In contrast, American Christians have often found themselves in positions of privilege in American society. However, the temptation to withdraw from the world has still presented itself to both twentieth- and twenty-first-century Christians in the United States. Similar to the self-view of Jerusalem in Lamentations 1:1-3, American Christians hold an elevated view of themselves. Into the twentieth century, the American church would claim an exceptional status in American society as well as believing in an exceptional status for the United States. However, challenges to the assumption of exceptionalism in the twentieth century would lead to the desire for the church to withdraw from society (similar to the temptation confronting God's people in Jeremiah 29:4-7).

At the onset of the twentieth century, optimism reigned over the possibility of the church's role in society.[4] For much of American history, the Protestant church held the belief in America's role as the city set on a hill, shining the light of Christ to all nations. Marsden describes the ethos of the American church in the first two decades of the twentieth century: "Success and progress still seemed the dominant mood, underlined by much rhetoric about unity, together with activism, and by beating the drums for the latest crusade."[5] Hope for a Christian century reigned over American Christianity.

By the end of the first third of the twentieth century, this optimism would be severely compromised. While theological liberals continued to hold a more optimistic view of American society,[6] the fundamentalist stream that helped form evangelicalism moved

away from such optimism. Theological conservatives in the middle
of the twentieth century leaned toward a more pessimistic view of
the role of the church in society. Disheartened by a perceived sense
of rejection by American society (particularly following the public
embarrassment of the Scopes trial), fundamentalists retreated from
American society.

Dispensational eschatology provided additional fodder for fundamentalist separatism. As Randall Balmer posits:

> Evangelicals suddenly felt their hegemonic hold over American
> society slipping away. . . . The teeming, squalid ghettoes, . . .
> festering with labor unrest, no longer resembled the precincts
> of Zion that postmillennial evangelicals had envisioned earlier
> in the century. . . . Faced with this wretchedness, American
> evangelicals looked to alter their eschatology.[7]

Dispensational eschatology, which envisioned the current epoch of
world history as only befitting judgment and destruction, fit this
worldview. It asserted that the last days of this world could not be
redeemed and that we were simply waiting for the destruction of
this world and the institution of the next world. The current world,
particularly the urban centers, had become uninhabitable for the
good Christian. This increasing pessimism over American cities
coincided with the influx of former slaves migrating from the Mis-
sissippi Delta to the northern cities and the increased number of
non-Protestant immigrants from southern and eastern Europe.
Rapid industrialization and the changing face of the urban landscape resulted in an increasingly negative view of cities and of society. White Protestant flight from the city, therefore, became the
solution for those fearful of such change.

The negative perception of a changed city aligned with dispensational eschatology. A drastic change from above would be required to stop the flood of secularism and societal decay.

> With their embrace of dispensationalism, evangelicals shifted
> their focus radically from social amelioration to individual re-
> generation. Having diverted their attention from the con-
> struction of the millennial realm, evangelicals concentrated on
> the salvation of souls and, in so doing, neglected reform efforts.[8]

An individualistic soul-saving soteriology emerged from a dispensational theology.

Theologically conservative Christians had shifted their priority
from concern for both the individual and larger society to more
exclusively a concern for the individual, and the first half of the
twentieth century witnessed the formation of this shift. In *The
Great Reversal*, David Moberg asserts that "there was a time when
evangelicals had a balanced position that gave proper attention to
both evangelism and social concern, but a great reversal in the
[twentieth] century led to a lopsided emphasis upon evangelism
and omission of most aspects of social involvement."[9] Marsden
notes that "the 'Great Reversal' took place from about 1900 to about
1930, when all progressive social concern, whether political or
private, became suspect among revivalist evangelicals and was relegated to a very minor role."[10]

Fundamentalists developed a suspicion about social engagement
and withdrew from social concerns spurred by their rejection of
larger society. This rejection of secular culture arose from anxiety
about the changes that occurred in the early part of the twentieth
century when fundamentalists felt they were under siege from
secular society. Marsden recognizes that "fundamentalism was the
response of traditionalist evangelicals who declared war on these
modernizing trends. In fundamentalist eyes the war had to be all-
out and fought on several fronts. At stake was nothing less than the
gospel of Jesus' blood and righteousness."[11] The twentieth century
witnessed fearful white Protestants yielding to the temptation to

withdraw from the city and engaging in the exact opposite behavior demanded by Jeremiah 29:7 to "seek the peace and prosperity of the city to which I have carried you into exile." There was an intentional abandonment of the city in favor of safety and comfort. Jerusalem was to be rebuilt in the suburbs.

Having lost their standing in society, fundamentalists of the early twentieth century would view their experience in society as paralleling the description of Lamentations 1:1-3. A sense of being exiled (in this case, a self-imposed exile) would envelop the conservative Protestant worldview. They saw themselves as a people once great among the nations or other faiths (v. 1); with many friends, lovers or at least admirers (v. 2); and experiencing affliction or a form of persecution from the hostile world (v. 3). In their self-perceived fall from power, twentieth-century fundamentalists claimed to empathize with the fall of Jerusalem. Throughout the twentieth century, they (and their ecclesial kin, the evangelicals) would engage a narrative of decline. This perception of being under siege and in decline created the same temptation confronting the exiles in Jeremiah 29: to withdraw from an increasingly hostile world.

If Jeremiah 29 first reveals the temptation to disengage from the city, the second temptation warns against acquiescing to the society in which they now live. The people of God are tempted to listen to false prophets who would tell them what they want to hear, rather than speak the actual heart and words of God. Jeremiah 29:8-9 asserts:

> Yes, this is what the LORD Almighty, the God of Israel, says:
> "Do not let the prophets and diviners among you deceive you.
> Do not listen to the dreams you encourage them to have. They
> are prophesying lies to you in my name. I have not sent them,"
> declares the LORD.

Jeremiah refers to false prophets who claimed that the exile would be short-lived and that Jerusalem would soon be restored. J. A. Thompson observes that "the false prophets had told the people that their stay would be short, and Jeremiah needed to assert that this was a falsehood . . . [the false prophets] were associates of diviners and dreamers (27:9). . . . It was an attempt to speed up the divine purposes. But Yahweh will not be hurried in his plans for his people."[12]

The exiles wanted to embrace the false prophets' offer of a quick resolution to their suffering, but these claims were made using the idolatrous practices of the times: divination and magic. Divination practices were "closely associated with various forms of magic and sorcery."[13] Divination reflects a desire to know and control the future by removing uncertainty. So Jeremiah confronts the work of those who attempt to foretell an optimistic future through idolatrous and magical means rather than speaking the words of YHWH.

For a people lacking hope in exile, the false prophets would tempt them with self-serving prophecies of palatable answers. The false prophets would give the people what they wanted. The false prophets would offer a simple and uncomplicated option for God's people. They would operate like vending machines. A vending machine offers a high degree of certainty—you get what you want. Insert a certain amount of money, punch a few buttons, and a specific product will appear. Israel longed for the specific answer that their exile would be short-lived. The false prophets offered the exact product desired by God's people, even if the product was not good for them.

Peter Steinke identifies this temptation as magic.

> Many are drawn to magic because of its promise of quickness. Before you know it—Presto! Repeat the cant "Abracadabra." Magic is not only quick but also direct. All sorcerers go for the end product, without the process. Here it is. No messy stuff. No questions. No confusing dialectic to toss and turn in your brain. It seems as if every magician possesses the master key to the door.[14]

YHWH worship, on the other hand, held no such promises. YHWH does not operate like a vending machine nor does he follow a simplistic pattern yielding the exact outcome we want. Defeated exiles would be tempted to forsake the complexity of YHWH worship for the simplicity of hearing exactly what they wanted to hear. In difficult times or times of great challenge, the people of God are tempted to believe solutions that are easy to follow because they align with what they desire. Jeremiah 29:8-9 presents a warning to the exiles to not give in to the temptation of the easy but false answers advocated by false prophets.

The same temptation to simple answers that Jeremiah 29 describes and Lamentations challenges is evident in American evangelical history. Following the flight of white Protestants from the cities in the twentieth century, the center of American Christian life shifted from the cities to the suburbs. Under the auspices that society had turned against them, conservative Christians deemed the city as a hostile environment, justifying white flight. White Christian flight, however, was attributable in no small part to the fear of nonwhite and non-Protestant migration into the urban centers. It was a time of uncertainty for many white American Christians, and the cities—now filled with "strangers"—were no longer what they had hoped for. Answers were needed.

The communities that moved to the suburbs embraced a narrative of church growth that reflected what they wanted to hear: affirmation that they made the right choice in fleeing the cities. The American church growth movement of the twentieth century provided the fuel for the development of a suburban church success formula and the concomitant development of a triumphalistic narrative for American evangelicalism. Suburban churches developed formulas for ministry that worked to great effect in the individualistic and consumeristic culture of suburban America. In other words, the suburban churches were told what they wanted to hear. It was right for them to have moved to the suburbs, because now their churches could grow and flourish. The churches in turn continued to offer answers and solutions that worked for the suburban families in attendance. The suburban churches embraced the pragmatism and applicability of church growth principles. This movement, popular in white suburban churches in the latter half of the twentieth century, adapted business and marketing principles in order to appeal to the masses and spread the word.[15]

American evangelicalism has created the unique phenomenon of church shopping—viewing church as yet another commodity and product to be evaluated and purchased. When a Christian family moves to a new city, how much of the standards by which they choose a church is based upon a shopping list of their personal tastes and wants rather than their commitment to a particular community or their desire to serve a particular neighborhood? Churches, in turn, have adapted their ministries to appeal to the consumer mindset of the American public.[16]

Pastoral leadership in the church relied on business models of strong leadership over biblical values of servant leadership. The practical, workable and easily applied formulas triggered the wide dissemination of church growth principles and contributed to the furthering of a materialistic and consumeristic church.

Churches in the suburbs heard what they wanted to hear, embracing a narrative of growth for the suburban church that affirmed their status. The challenge of Jeremiah 29:8-9 went unheeded by the twentieth-century American evangelical church as it embraced the palatable message of a worldly ecclesiology of easy-to-hear and simple-to-apply concepts and principles.

The burgeoning suburban megachurches offered formulas to follow that ensured success for other churches. Barbara Ehrenreich notes that "some of the more successful megachurches . . . have

spawned ancillary businesses as church growth consultancies themselves, offering training seminars, websites, and conferences for the
pastors of lesser churches."[17] The church growth movement applied
in the suburban context called for the formation of ministry arising
from a market economy, becoming a fully capitalistic venture. In
Holy Mavericks, Shayne Lee and Phil Sinitiere reveal that

> religious suppliers thrive in a competitive spiritual marketplace
> because they are quick, decisive, and flexible in reacting to
> changing conditions, savvy at packaging and marketing their
> ministries, and resourceful at offering spiritual rewards that
> resonate with the existential needs and cultural tastes of the
> public.[18]

Market-savvy individuals rose to prominence and influence by ex-
ploiting the spiritual marketplace.

The church growth movement chiefly expressed through white
suburban churches reveals a "can do" attitude belying cultural triumphalism, and this emerges as a central narrative of evangelicalism.
Ehrenreich notes that proponents of the contemporary church
growth movement emerged from a positive-thinking approach. She
observes that church growth proponents are exemplified by a belief
that "a church gets big because its spirit is big. . . . Nobody ever
started a business without hoping that someday, if he or she worked
hard enough, it would be a big success. That is the American dream,
isn't it?"[19] This belief that human effort could conquer the problems
of the church coupled with positive thinking began to shape the
evangelical ethos.

There is no shortage of magic formulas that appeal to the masses.
The message of easy answers from the false prophets of Jeremiah
29:8-9 is still available in the twenty-first century. Simple solutions
present a persistent temptation for the pastor. Frustrated pastors,
weary of waiting for their church to turn around, will have no problem

accessing resources with the latest and greatest idea. American churches are not supposed to struggle, and they are not supposed to decline, so we believe American ingenuity and know-how will solve these problems. There are always simple answers if we want to hear them. But Jeremiah 29 challenges these presuppositions and the simple solutions that tickle the ear of the typical American pastor. It is the same message that so many American Christians want to hear: they are still in control, there is no need for judgment, and there is no suffering. But easy answers that offer false hope are not solutions.

Jeremiah 29 opposes two of the options available to the exiles. They should not withdraw and hide from life in the city (even in the heart of the wicked city of Babylon); nor should they listen to the answers they want to hear—the simple solutions—from the false prophets. The passage challenges the church to be salt and light to the world (Mt 5:13-16). By rejecting these two key temptations, the acceptable alternative becomes lament. Withdrawal from the world or accepting simplistic answers reveals human effort or human problem solving, while lament acknowledges who is ultimately in control. In the midst of a crisis, Lamentations points toward God and acknowledges his sovereignty regardless of the circumstances.

Lamentations 1:1-3 reminds us of Jerusalem's story by contrasting the past glory with the anguish of the present crisis. A dramatic change of fortune is demonstrated. The reality of this destruction presents the challenge of the book of Lamentations. How will God's people respond? Will they only look for the answers they want to hear? Will they run and hide, or will they enter into the place of lament and embrace the reality of their situation? The historical context of the fall of Jerusalem as revealed in Lamentations 1:1-3 and Jeremiah 29:4-9 points to the necessity of Lamentations. By challenging the two primary temptations facing the exiles, Scripture now points the people of God toward the proper response to a broken world: lament.

The Funeral Dirge

The Genre of Lament

Lament serves a multitude of functions reflected by the various genres and forms. As Westermann notes, "the lament has a history. . . . [It] has a historical antecedent."[1] Lament, therefore, recounts a historical *suffering*. "Lament stems from an acute experience of pain, be it physical, emotional, or spiritual."[2] It is the human response to anguish and adversity, and is not bound by the rules of praise. Instead, lament can take the form of complaint, "in the sense of bemoaning the troubles one has undergone . . . [and] complaint in the sense of arguing with and complaining to God about one's situation and protesting its continuation."[3] Lament is an act of protest as the lamenter is allowed to express indignation and even outrage about the experience of suffering. The lamenter talks back to God and ultimately petitions him for help, in the midst of pain. The one who laments can call out to God for help, and in that outcry there is the hope and even the manifestation of praise.

In the book of Lamentations, we encounter the breadth of the various forms of lament. In the first chapter, we find a particular form of lament with many of the above characteristics: the funeral dirge. The funeral dirge deals with the historical reality of a suffering community that raises voices of pain and protest over the death of Jerusalem.

Jeremiah 29 addresses the exiles in Babylon, while Lamentations is written to the remnant in Jerusalem. The exiles in Babylon are susceptible to false prophets who promise them what they want to hear: the hope that they will soon return to Jerusalem. To them, the devastation of Jerusalem is a physically distant reality. However, those remaining in Jerusalem are confronted with the painful and visible reality at hand. Lamentations is written to this remnant who witnessed this devastation. A funeral dirge is necessary because the dead body of the city lies before them.

Chapter 1 (as well as chapters 2 and 4) opens with the Hebrew word *'eka*, translated into English as "alas" or "how." A more dynamic translation could yield "how tragic" or "how devastated." A confused cry of anguish, "How can this be?" is offered in response to a tragic death. The opening word reflects an emotional reaction. "Tragedy threatens to overcome speech, sobs interfere with words."[4] This opening cry of desolation acknowledges that Lamentations occurs in the context of tragedy. The city has died and the people must respond with lament.

Kathleen O'Connor summarizes the key characteristics of a funeral dirge, which "include a mournful cry for the one who has died, a proclamation of death, contrast with previous circumstances of the dead person, and the reaction of bystanders."[5] Lamentations 1 laments a death "but with national rather than personal application."[6] There is an opening mournful cry of *'eka* (v. 1) over the death of Jerusalem. There is a proclamation of the death as the city sits alone (v. 1), with references to widowhood (v. 1); descriptions of mourning, grief, bitter anguish (v. 4); being crushed/trampled (v. 15); the priests and elders have perished (v. 19); and "there is only death" (v. 20). This reality contrasts to previous circumstances when Jerusalem "once was great among the nations" and a "queen"

(v. 1), with references to a former glory marked by appointed feasts (v. 4), splendor (v. 6) and treasures (vv. 7, 10). Finally, there is the reaction of the bystanders with "no one to comfort her. All her friends have betrayed her; they have become her enemies" (v. 2). The absence of a comforter is restated in verses 9, 16, 17 and 21. Not only does no one comfort her, but the bystanders respond with betrayal (vv. 2, 19) and derisive laughter (v. 7)—they despise her (v. 11) and rejoice at her suffering (v. 21). The major characteristics of the funeral dirge are evident in Lamentations 1. As the first poem recounts this painful reality of the death of Jerusalem, the appropriate response is to engage in the practice of the funeral dirge.

Lamentations 1 deals with reality; lament is required because of the historic event of the death of the city and the nation. Lamentations serves as "an outpouring of grief for a loss that has already occurred, with no expectation of reversing that loss. . . . [The prophets] saw the demise of the nation as a *fait accompli*. They personify the nation as a corpse, over whom a dirge is recited."[7] Lamentations 1 reflects a postmortem grief over death rather than an anxiety over the future possible death of the city. It is not the moment to explain or justify. It is not even a moment to plead for a better future. Lamentations 1 provides the space and time to mourn. The funeral dirge does not allow for the denial of death, nor does it allow for the denial of culpability in that death. The funeral dirge is a reality check for those who witness suffering and allows mourning that is essential for dealing with death.

Rather than denying reality, Lamentations portrays suffering and death in gritty detail. Lamentations 1 uncompromisingly describes the true status of the situation. Even if God's people wanted to close their eyes and shut out the suffering around them, Lamentations won't allow it. Slavery (v. 1), abandonment (v. 2), affliction (vv. 3, 9), harsh labor (v. 3), distress (v. 3), anguish (v. 4), suffering (v. 5), violation, shame (v. 7), being despised (v. 11), desolation (vv. 13, 16), being faint (v. 13), being trodden over and crushed (v. 15), torment (v. 20) and death (v. 20) are not glossed over. Even the cringe-worthy description of being naked (v. 8) and filthy in her skirts (v. 9) (with connotations of sexual and possibly menstrual uncleanness) and an allusion to sexual violation (v. 10) is presented in stark terms. The vivid description does not allow for the denial of suffering and death, nor does it allow for the denial of culpability. The funeral dirge recognizes suffering but also recognizes sinful behavior that contributed to that suffering.

Lament is honesty before God and each other. If something has truly been declared dead, there is no use in sugarcoating that reality. To hide from suffering and death would be an act of denial. If an individual would deny the reality of death during a funeral, friends would justifiably express concern over the mental health of that individual. In the same way, should we not be concerned over a church that lives in denial over the reality of death in our midst?

Our nation's tainted racial history reflects a serious inability to deal with reality. Something has died and we refuse to participate in the funeral. We refuse to acknowledge the lamenters who sing the songs of suffering in our midst. In *Forgive Us*, my coauthors and I confront the inability of the American church to deal with historical reality. We fail to acknowledge the reality of sins committed by the church and fail to offer a moral witness to the world. Ibrahim Abdul-Matin addresses this deficiency in our culture, stating that "People of faith have lost their moral authority . . . because they have lacked humility: they have failed to acknowledge the ways they are part of the problem."[8] The funeral dirge opening of Lamentations and the first three verses of Lamentations 1 remind us that grief that emerges from a very real and painful history must be acknowledged.

Self-absorbed Christians who are apathetic toward injustice do not emerge from a vacuum. A deeply segregated church does not appear without history. In the United States, grief and pain related to race are often suppressed, and the stories of suffering are often untold. Our history is incomplete. The painful stories of the suffering of the African American community, in particular, remain hidden. Often, American Christians may even deny the narrative of suffering, claiming that things weren't so bad for the slaves or that at least the African Americans had the chance to convert to Christianity. The story of suffering is often swept under the rug in order not to create discomfort or bad feelings. Lament is denied because the dead body in front of us is being denied. But the funeral dirge genre of Lamentations 1 requires the telling of the full story of death—the cause of that death, the history surrounding that death and the historical effects of that death—because a dead body cannot be ignored.

The slave trade that brought Africans to the Western Hemisphere brutally stripped them of all identity, resulting in the complete obliteration of kinship, family, identity and history. The subsequent history of the progeny of the African slaves in the United States has stifled their story. In the church, there is a particular absence of knowledge about the stories of the African American church. Western theological history dominates while the stories of slave religion are left untold. Spirituality in the African American church is assumed to be an essential internal characteristic, negating the need to more fully understand its nuances.

Several years ago, I attended a conference on ancient-future faith that emphasized the importance of engaging ancient spirituality in contemporary expressions of Christian faith. This conference promoted seventeenth- and eighteenth-century hymns as an example of "ancient" faith, but failed to mention even once the spirituality of the early Christian slave community that dates several centuries earlier.[9] A theological reading of Lamentations 1 as a funeral dirge calls the church to make room for the stories of suffering. Space is created for racial healing to arise from the power of stories, particularly stories of suffering. So Lamentations begins with a funeral dirge; before any answers are offered, a postmortem must be offered.

Willie Jennings notes that the first European slave ship that arrived in Africa was under the command of Henry, the Christian prince of Portugal. When the slaves were brought to the shore to be taken into the hold of the ship,

> Prince Henry, following his deepest Christian instincts, ordered a tithe to be given to God through the church. . . . This act of praise and thanksgiving to God . . . served to justify the royal rhetoric by which Prince Henry claimed his motivation was the salvation of the soul of the heathen.[10]

In 1444, that first European slave ship operated under the faulty assumption that their actions were ordained by God. This warped belief continued, allowing slave traders to justify their sinful actions.

The slave ship served to reshape the imagination of all involved. "Everyone who stepped on a slave ship became racialized, white and black."[11] The crew would participate in the dehumanizing of the slaves. "Those who resisted in any way were beaten or whipped without mercy. . . . The rape of black women was woven into the very fabric of the social order of the slave ship . . . as sailors shared fully in the brutal rape and torture of women and children."[12] The slave ship's arrival into port meant the transfer from one place of torture to a new place of torture. The auction bell that would greet the slave ship would signal the transition to life on the plantation.

On the plantation, some semblance of family life was initiated. However, the slave masters regularly employed rape as a weapon, inflicting significant pain and spiritual suffering on slave women. The slave system "used their bodies for breeding and their bloodline for the maintenance of racial order. . . . In the eyes of the slave holders, slave women . . . were simply instruments guaranteeing the growth of the slave labor force."[13] Slave women were constant victims of rape by white slave masters. The system of slavery was a system deeply rooted in spiritual evil that brought death to its victims. These stories reveal a deep flaw in our nation's story. Human bodies were not treated as made in the image of God. These bodies and their stories remain buried in our national narrative.

Lamentations 1 provides a truthful telling of the dead body in the room. The tragedy of our racial history requires the lament of a funeral dirge. What potential healing could occur if we were to take the example of Lamentations 1 in necessary truth telling? The city is deserted and the queen has become a slave. Affliction and harsh labor are a part of the reality. How could *we* benefit from a funeral dirge that calls us to an honest depiction of the dead body in the room?

A few years ago I was presenting a workshop on the topic of lament. I raised the importance of telling the whole story of slavery in order to engage in the fullness of lament and how the funeral dirge of Lamentations 1 offers the possibility of healing as we deal with the truth. As part of the presentation I narrated an account of plantation life, in particular, the horrific account of the sexual abuse of slave women. One of my good friends happened to be in the workshop listening to me read the account. When I began to describe the atrocities of rape on the plantation, my friend got up and stood in the back of the room. For the following fifteen minutes, the duration of my workshop, he remained standing. Even after the workshop ended and all of the participants had left the room, he remained.

I approached him as he silently stood in the back of the room. I began to mutter some sort of apology, but he stopped me in the middle of my sentence. "When there were five kids in the slave family, there was the one kid that was lighter than the rest of the kids. That's my family. That's my family's story. You told my family's story. I have not heard another tell my story in public like that before, and I needed to honor you by standing." There is power in bringing untold stories to light. The freedom to speak about the reality of suffering and death results in a freedom from denial. Lamentations 1 presents as a funeral dirge to remind us that we cannot ignore what is right in front of us.

In the American Christian narrative, the stories of the dominant culture are placed front and center while stories from the margins are often ignored. As we rush toward a description of an America that is now postracial, we forget that the road to this phase is littered with dead bodies. There has been a deep and tragic loss in the American story because we have not acknowledged the reality of death. Stories remain untold or ignored in our quest to "get over" it. But in the end, we have lost an important part of who we are as a nation and as a church. We have yet to engage in a proper funeral dirge for our tainted racial history and continue to deny the deep spiritual stronghold of a nation that sought to justify slavery.

The tragedies of the slave trade and the long-term establishment of a slave society have no biblical rationalization and justification. No amount of intellectual gymnastics can justify this atrocity by claiming that there is a redemptive muscular Christianity inherent in the warped value system of a slave society. No amount of scriptural twisting can justify the brutal treatment of human beings made in the image of God. The history of the transatlantic slave trade points to a deeply problematic and dysfunctional Christian imagination that contributed to its rise. By not acknowledging this very real death, we ignore the implication of the funeral dirge in Lamentations. We do not recognize the stench of a dead body in the room.

The funeral dirge genre employed throughout the book of Lamentations and presented in chapter 1 acknowledges reality. The tragic death that has occurred cannot be easily dismissed. The painful story is expressed and allows the one who suffers to express grief. In the same way, the painful stories in American history must be revealed and learned. Racial reconciliation requires the truth telling of the funeral dirge lament and the expression of grief.

The funeral dirge of Lamentations allowed for a vivid, honest description of reality. A contemporary funeral dirge for the twenty-first-century American church would require the effort to more fully understand and learn another's history. It could be as simple as watching films that depict the atrocities of the slave trade and the institution of slavery. It may involve visiting museums that teach the history of racism in the United States. It may require a deepening understanding by reading texts that engage this often-hidden history. The knowledge of this history can begin the process toward an authentic lament. The church must engage in a funeral dirge that reflects the truth of our tainted history.

Silenced Voices of Shame

Lamentations 1:1-22

In Lamentations 1, we encounter two different voices. The first voice rises from an unidentified observer/prophet who reflects on Jerusalem's suffering. This narrator who appears throughout the book initially speaks in verses 1:1-11, 17. While there is some debate about the identity of the author, many agree with Norman Gottwald that "the traditional author is the prophet Jeremiah."[1] Second Chronicles 35:25 states that "Jeremiah composed laments for Josiah, and to this day all the male and female singers commemorate Josiah in the laments. These became a tradition in Israel and are written in the Laments." The preface to Lamentations in the Septuagint (the Greek Old Testament) reads: "And it came to pass after the captivity of Israel and the desolation of Jerusalem that Jeremiah sat mourning and he lamented this lament over Jerusalem."

Most of the able-bodied leaders and influencers had been sent into exile at the time of Lamentations' writing. Jeremiah, as one who supported surrender to the Babylonians, would probably have been spared and would therefore be a witness to the destruction of Jerusalem. While Jeremiah is never explicitly named as the author, we can move toward the interpretation that when the narrator appears in Lamentations, he offers Jeremiah's perspective as a key prophet (possibly the only prophet remaining) in Jerusalem after the exile.

The second voice speaks as Jerusalem personified as a suffering woman. "Although the narrator is the book's first speaker . . . he is a distant observer, an 'objective' reporter. . . . His distance and lack of passion contribute to her abandonment."[2] O'Connor notes that "the narrator is unemotional; he coolly describes the city woman's plight and is obsessed with her lost glory."[3] The personified voice of Jerusalem identified as Daughter Zion (v. 6) speaks in the first person and serves as a more personal voice, directly involved in the experience and narrative of suffering (vv. 9, 11-22). "Emotion overwhelms Daughter Zion, who complains only of her present pain."[4] "Look, LORD, on my affliction (v. 9); I am despised (v. 11); Is any suffering like my suffering that was inflicted on me, that the LORD brought on me? (v. 12); [Daughter Zion speaks of YHWH who] sent fire . . . into my bones (v. 13)." In a highly personalized way, Jerusalem speaks of a deep pain and suffering.

The personification of Jerusalem helps the listener/reader engage with the suffering on both a corporate and individual level. Knut Heim observes that "personification helps to conceptualize and verbalize pain. . . . Furthermore, the projection of personal and communal experience ('I' and 'we'/'you' [plural]) onto a third person ('she') helps the individual and the community to structure their own experience of themselves."[5] In contrast to the impersonal narrator who maintains an emotional distance, the personified voice of Jerusalem draws us into a more direct experience of suffering and the shame that accompanies suffering. Instead of an impersonal, abstract idea of the city, we encounter the sense of very real suffering by an individual, even as that individual speaks a personified account of a corporate experience. "Personification helps the grieving process by unlocking the inner thoughts of the suffering individuals, breaking the boundaries of privacy."[6] Suffering moves from the impersonal to the personal. The shame felt by Jerusalem is intensified when it is seen through the lens of a direct personal experience.

Jerusalem's personification as an adulterous woman who is unfaithful toward her husband YHWH amplifies the feeling of shame and suffering. In other portions of the Old Testament, Israel is portrayed as God's bride. YHWH entered into a covenant of marriage with Israel and Jerusalem (Is 54:5; 62:5; Jer 31:32; Ezra 16:8, 60; Hos 2:7). Israel's early devotion to YHWH (Jer 2:2; Hos 2:15) contrasts to her "many sins" (Lam 1:5) and how "Jerusalem has sinned greatly and so has become unclean" (Lam 1:8). Delbert Hillers translates the second half of verse 8 as, "the people shake their heads at her, . . . i.e., [she has become an] 'object of scorn.'"[7]

The covenant of marriage has been violated by Jerusalem. "The narrator implies that she is an adulterer (1:8-9)."[8] She has been unfaithful to her husband, YHWH. Adele Berlin points out that in verses 8-10: "Just as her sin is expressed in the sexual terms of unfaithfulness and adultery, so her shame is expressed in the sexual terms of nakedness (sexual disgrace) and sexual abuse. . . . Jerusalem is the object of derision and shame."[9] Jerusalem's impurity and infidelity is implied in the abandonment by her lovers (v. 2). She "has become unclean" and "all who honored her despise her, for they have all seen her naked. . . . Her filthiness clung to her skirts" (vv. 8, 9).

The explicit language in these verses points to a deep sense of shame, amplified by the cultural context of Lamentations. "Exposure of one's body, especially the genitals, was to the ancient Israelites an almost immeasurable disgrace, a shame they felt much more deeply than most moderns would."[10] Exposure and nakedness is a precursor to the further shame and suffering to follow. The language in this section evokes the image of Jerusalem as a sexually assaulted woman. The image of the enemy's hands stretched out all over her precious things (v. 10) appears to be a euphemism for sexual assault. Jerusalem's suffering can be attributed to her infidelity in taking lovers (v. 2), but the shame culminates in an undeserved mistreatment and sexual assault by her conquerors. The description of Jerusalem's shame as sexual shame heightens the visceral, bodily shame felt by God's people.

SIN, SHAME AND *HAN*

The self-assessment of shame acknowledged by God's people is part of the process of lament. There is an honest, if not a brutal description of Jerusalem's shame. Lament is deeply *felt.* It is not simply a conscious, cognitive exercise. Feelings of shame generate the desire to cover up in contrast to the exposure that occurs. The shamed person wants to hide, but in Lamentations 1, there is no place to hide. This feeling of shame is exasperated by the public exposure and the response of others toward that shame. Jerusalem notes that "my sins have been bound into a yoke. . . . They have been hung on my neck" (v. 14), resulting in Jerusalem becoming "an unclean thing" (v. 17). The image of an unclean thing may allude to a menstrual rag, which would be evidence of her ritual impurity and makes "her shame vivid, graphic and repulsive. It also underscores her isolation—she is untouchable and without a comforter."[11] In Lamentations the depth of Jerusalem's shame is amplified by the public exposure of that shame and the corresponding isolation that comes from public shame. Recognizing that shame, however, becomes an essential aspect of lament. Shame cannot be explained away; it must be addressed.

The Western view of sin tends to limit our understanding to the guilt of the individual who commits the sin, but this is not the only perspective on sin offered in Lamentations. Jerusalem's experience outlined in Lamentations 1 points to the guilt of her sinful acts but also reveals how Jerusalem has been ravaged by sin and the subsequent shame that emerges.

Andrew Park's perspective on the theological concept of *han* arising from the Korean context provides insight into the experience of Jerusalem in Lamentations. Park defines sin as "the wrongdoing of people toward God and their neighbors. *Han* is the pain experienced by the victimized neighbors. Sin is the unjust act of the oppressors; *han* the passive experience of their victims."[12] Korean theologian Young-Hak Hyun further defines *han* as "a sense of unresolved resentment against injustice suffered, . . . a feeling of acute pain of sorrow in one's guts and bowels."[13] Park's distinction between sin and *han* points to the seeming incongruity of the depiction of Jerusalem as simultaneously the sinful adulterer and the victim of sexual assault.

The language of sin as used by Western Christianity does not provide the necessary nuance to understand how a victim of sin experiences sin. "Traditional theology has emphasized one-sidedly the sin of all people, while ignoring the pain of the victim. Its doctrine of sin must be complemented by dealing with the suffering of the victim."[14] The shame experienced by Jerusalem cannot be addressed with the same methodology used to address individual guilt.

Western concepts of sin lead us to feel guilty when we do something bad, but we often do not have the language of shame when we are sinned against. When the shame of *han* overwhelms us, as it does the personified Jerusalem in Lamentations, the simple act of individual confession does not prove adequate. *Han* must be addressed on the level in which it operates. Andrew Park suggests "that with a vision of new relationships or the Hanless society, we confront the Han-causing elements and transform them."[15] The guilt of individual sin leads to individual confession, but the shame of *han* should lead to social transformation.

As previously stated, Americans often have a difficult time addressing the issue of race. The tendency in the dialogue on race in the United States contrasts to the acknowledgment of shame in the book of Lamentations. American culture tends to hide the stories of guilt and shame and seeks to elevate stories of success. American culture gravitates toward narratives of exceptionalism and triumphalism, which results in amnesia about a tainted history. The reality of a shameful history undermines the narrative of exceptionalism, so it must remain hidden.

Social psychologist Brené Brown summarizes this tendency in explaining our inability to engage in a conversation on race: "You cannot have that conversation without shame, because you cannot talk about race without talking about privilege. And when people start talking about privilege, they get paralyzed by shame."[16] True reconciliation, justice and *shalom* require a remembering of suffering, an unearthing of a shameful history and a willingness to enter into lament. Lament calls for an authentic encounter with the truth and challenges privilege, because privilege would hide the truth that creates discomfort.

The primary narrative that forms our ministry models draws from our evangelical success stories. We are presented with triumphalistic narratives that minimize stories of struggle. Our historical reflection reveals an obsession with success and celebration while stories of survival and suffering are ignored. History is often told by the victorious and therefore favors them. In *Mirror to the Church*, Emmanuel Katongole challenges the church to reflect on the full scope of history.

> Without the history, . . . assessments of the situation easily turned into a blame game between warring parties. . . . As we seek to understand the stories that shape us, it is important to name the silence of history in so many of the stories we tell. . . . There is a history that we have to account for. When we don't, it is easy to assume that things such as tribe, race, and terrorism are natural, or simply the way things are.[17]

The depth of pain endemic to racial hostility requires full disclosure for complete healing. The church should become the place where the fullness of suffering is expressed in a safe environment. Liturgy, worship, leadership, small groups and other aspects of church life should provide the safe place where the fullness of suffering can be set free. Stories of suffering can never be buried when lament is an important and central aspect of the church's worship life. Lamentations reminds us that the proper response to tragedy and suffering is lament. The persistent history of shame in our story as a church requires the type of lament offered in Lamentations. This shame may be isolating, but it is essential to the honesty that is required in lament.

GENDER AND SILENCED VOICES

The personification of Jerusalem as a woman has a theological intent. Not only does the feminine voice of Jerusalem allude to Israel's history as God's bride who has committed adultery, but it also provides insight into the shame of abuse and assault that is perpetrated upon a woman. Expressing a theology of celebration in the context of victory and success would lend itself to a voice of triumph reflecting a culturally masculine voice. A theology of suffering in the context of pain would call for a culturally feminine voice. Much of the suffering in Lamentations reflects a woman's voice, beginning in chapter 1 with the feminine personification of Jerusalem as one who has experienced tremendous suffering and pain. Kathleen O'Connor states that "the poetry focuses on her (Zion's) female roles—widow, mother, lover, and rape victim. . . . By making Jerusalem a woman, the poetry gives her personality and human characteristics that evoke pity or disdain from readers."[18] Lamentations may prove to be the most important book of the bible with a dominant feminine voice.

The image of a woman in great pain evokes an emotional response to the poetry of Lamentations 1. "Daughter Zion speaks from within the trauma. Her first-person statements carry the power of experience and the cascading confusion of a survivor."[19] Jerusalem is a widow who has become a slave (v. 1). Jerusalem weeps bitter tears with no one to comfort her and with no resting place (vv. 2, 3). The young women grieve and Jerusalem is in bitter anguish (v. 4). She experiences grief (v. 5), and her splendor has departed (v. 6). In verse 7, Jerusalem experiences a strong sense of helplessness, wandering and isolation. Some commentators believe that the uncleanness and filthiness of verses 8 and 9 may refer to the menstrual cycle. Images of sexual assault make up verse 10. The images of widowhood (v. 1), mothers who have lost their children (v. 16), and a sense of profound alienation (v. 12) and helplessness in the face of great external oppressions dominate the first chapter of Lamentations. In the face of this tremendous suffering, women's voices rise up to express the depth of sorrow experienced by the community.

The voices of suffering women in the book of Lamentations offer an important counternarrative to the triumphalistic tendencies of God's people in the United States. We are likely to tune out the stories of suffering and struggle that undermine our success narratives, in contrast to the women's voices in Lamentations 1 that rise up to speak truth when experiencing a painful reality. Instead, our ears are tuned to hear what we want to hear, similar to the exiles who listen to the false prophets in Jeremiah 29.

American evangelical inability to move beyond Christian triumphalism arises from the inability to hear voices outside the dominant white male narrative. Evangelical Christians who fail to hear the crucial voice of women can easily ignore critical elements of the biblical story, revealing a deep insensitivity to the reality of a suffering world. In the 2012 US elections, several male candidates lost their congressional races after making horribly insensitive comments about rape. Partisan politics is not the issue under discussion here. The problem arose from the inability to sufficiently empathize and authentically reflect the stories of women.

In recent years, the attempt to silence the voices of women in the church reflects a severe loss for the church. The dominant male voices have dictated the rules of acceptable conduct for evangelical leadership. The dominant ethos of evangelicalism has reflected this overwhelmingly male perspective. The evangelical use of silly and inappropriate terms like "muscular Christianity" reveals a masculine insecurity. We gravitate toward the silly triumphalistic tendencies of an unfettered masculinity without the necessary balance of other voices found in the Bible, particularly evident in the book of Lamentations. How an individual reflects biblical masculinity should not be culturally derived or based upon the oppression and suppression of women. It saddens me to hear that in some evangelical circles, the assertion of male headship is considered central to the core tenet of Christian faith. This assertion of male primacy is seemingly placed on par with the divinity of Christ. Masculinity should not be based upon external cultural or social qualities. The desire to associate evangelical Christianity with a culturally warped form of masculinity reveals a culturally captive Christianity rather than a biblical one.

The book of Lamentations gives us a clear example of the necessity of women's voices among God's people. In these passages in Lamentations 1, women's voices stand front and center. Lamentations does not survive without the voice of women. Unfortunately, in recent years, the American evangelical community has attempted to silence the voices of women. By silencing these voices, we have an inadequate understanding of Lamentations and the biblical message as a whole. We assert a warped form of masculinity at the expense of hearing the whole story from all perspectives.

A few years ago my mom, now in her eighties, was diagnosed with early stages of dementia. As of this writing, a woman who has always possessed a sharp wit has begun to respond at an alarmingly slow rate. My mother has lived through a very difficult set of life circumstances. She endured a very difficult marriage. For most of her married life, her husband was not around, resulting in her raising four kids on her own as an immigrant in a foreign land. Her minimal

English skills as a first generation immigrant meant that she took minimum-wage jobs (often two at a time) to keep her family together. During one stretch, she worked two jobs: a day-shift job at an inner-city carry-out and the graveyard shift at an inner-city nursing home. She was working twenty hours a day, six days a week. Throughout all her trials, she never lost her faith. To this day, even with her eyesight failing her, she faithfully reads chapter after chapter of Scripture. She would wake up at dawn to pray for hours every day. Several years ago, I noticed that her knee caps had split into several pieces from many hours spent kneeling in prayer. When she kneels, her broken kneecaps conform to the flat surface of the floor.

My deep disappointment in American evangelicalism is that stories like hers are deemed less worthy than the stories of the latest evangelical superstar with a megachurch. My mother's story aligns with the tenor of the book of Lamentations. Her life story embodies a theology of lament. Lamentations 1 presents the voices of suffering women. Rather than presenting the triumphant voices of the male rulers, Lamentations presents the feminine voice. In contrast to Lamentations, American Christianity upholds a more worldly perspective on the value of individuals. We love to hear from the hotshot pastor with the hip haircut, tattoo and trendy style. The roster of evangelical conference speakers and the list of those deemed to be experts in ministry are dominated by white males.

Recently, I pointed out to a conference organizer that they were featuring twenty-nine white speakers and one nonwhite speaker at a missional conference. The organizer of the conference graciously asked me to submit names for their next conference. But he also stated that they didn't need any theological input because they already had people (by my deduction, they were all white males) who were working out missional theology. Evangelical conferences will elevate white male speakers, even if they have no direct experience or expertise on topics such as urban ministry and racial reconciliation.

A blog site that claims to focus on justice ministry has no articles by people of color out of its thirty articles under the category of "Reconciliation." Under the category of "Racism," the blog site features twelve posts authored by white males, one by a white female and one post by an Asian American author.[20] A website that streams videos considered crucial for evangelical ministers offers nine videos under the heading of "Cities" by white presenters and two videos with one white and one nonwhite copresenter.[21] Even on topics like racism and ministry in the cities, the experts are white males.

We worship at the altar of the latest and greatest American evangelical icons who regale us with stories of the exploits of their cutting-edge ministry. Our ears have been tuned to hear the call for successful pastors who will go and conquer the world with muscular Christianity, where celebration exists without lament. Meanwhile, we ignore the stories of suffering and oppression (often times the voices of women oppressed by their own communities). We have a deficient theology that trumpets the triumphalistic successes of evangelicalism while failing to hear from the stories of suffering that often tell us more about who we are as a community.

Having been a church planter and now teaching church planting at a seminary, I am often asked about the secret to successful church planting. Many current and future church planters will ask questions at pastors' conferences about what it takes to plant a church successfully. I will usually tell them that they should stop spending so much money attending these conferences to hear from individuals who don't really know more than them, whose secrets to success are really recipes for disaster. My "secret" to successful church planting is a praying mom and a praying spouse. In our church-planting efforts in Cambridge, I was very blessed to be surrounded by praying family members. Time spent attending the latest popular conference or reading the latest book on how to succeed as a church planter often proved to be wasted. In alignment with Ecclesiastes, there was really nothing new under the sun.

Instead of looking for success formulas derived from masculine triumphalism to build our churches, we should seek to understand the heart of prayer and lament. The evangelical machinery that churns out celebrities of successful pastors should be eschewed in light of a deeper spirituality that reflects a greater sensitivity and empathy. Our heroes should not be those who relish in masculine triumphalism but rather those whose hearts are tuned to the heart of God.

Often, the insights of women whose hearts are attuned to the heart of God are silenced because so much of our ministry endeavors arise from a culturally derived false sense of masculinity. Lamentations 1 points toward the power of the feminine voice in the biblical account. Lamentations 1 highlights the voice of suffering women as central to the experience of lament. We are forcing a theological famine upon ourselves by ignoring the voices of women. There is a deficiency in American evangelical ministry because we fail to reflect the feminine voice that is evident in portions of Scripture like Lamentations. This deficiency is to our great loss as a Christian community.

Comfort and Hope

The book of Lamentations expresses the deep pain and suffering of God's people. Lament dominates this moment in Israel's history. However, the primacy of lament in this book does not preclude the possibility of praise. Claus Westermann draws clear lines of distinction between the biblical genres of praise and lament, but he acknowledges the possibility of movement from lament to praise. Westermann writes that

> the beginnings and transitions to praise of God are seen even
> in the laments of the people and of the individual. Thus the

confession of confidence, which is in Israel such a meaningful and richly developed part, is not to be sharply separated from praise of God. Thus the vow of praise directly points the way to the Psalm of praise.[22]

He notes that "in the Psalms the lament is consistently followed by a petition, i.e., a supplication for help."[23] Lament leads to petition which leads to praise for God's response to the petition. Brueggemann summarizes that the power of lament is "that these psalms move from plea to praise. . . . The intervention of God in some way permits the move from plea to praise . . . [and] the proper setting of praise is as lament resolved."[24] While many individual and self-contained lament psalms may not provide an immediate, internal resolution, the entire book of Psalms provides a balanced account. The movement from lament to praise, therefore, can occur both within the psalm itself or the movement from one psalm to the next. Lament stands alone as a genre, but the Psalms as a whole strike a balance between the two genres.

Psalm 22 begins with "My God, my God, why have you forsaken me? / Why are you so far from saving me?" The psalm moves toward a plea that the LORD "not be far from me. / You are my strength; come quickly to help me. / Deliver me from the sword." The lament psalms end on hopeful notes of trust, signifying that "dominion belongs to the LORD / and he rules over the nations. . . . They will proclaim his righteousness, / declaring to a people yet unborn: / He has done it!" Even toward the end of Psalm 22, there is a movement from deep lament to profound praise, followed by a strong sense of confidence in God in Psalm 23. The images of God's provision dominate the familiar "The LORD is my Shepherd" psalm.

In similar fashion, Psalm 130, which begins with "Out of the depths I cry to you," moves to "so that we can, with reverence, serve you," culminating with "I wait for the LORD, my whole being waits, / and in his word I put my hope" and "He himself will redeem Israel / from all their sins." Lament serves the purpose of providing a necessary step toward praise. Psalm 131, a psalm of trust and a song of ascent, follows with images of contentment, "I have calmed and quieted myself," moving toward a call to worship from the entire community, "Israel, put your hope in the LORD / both now and forevermore."

Both the internal (within the psalm itself) content of the lament psalm and its external structure and arrangement reveal an expectation of trust and hope that leads to praise following the presentation of a plea rising out of lament. Praise, therefore, should follow lament. However, in a cultural context that upholds triumph and victory but fails to engage with suffering, praise *replaces* lament. We skip the important step of lament and offer supplication in a contextual vacuum. Praise, therefore, can seem hollow when neither lament nor petition has been sufficiently offered. Petition arises out of lament. The one who suffers brings the appropriate petition in view of the experience of lament.

Throughout the first chapter of Lamentations Jerusalem repeatedly states that there is no one to comfort her (vv. 2, 7, 9, 16, 17, 21). The lack of a comforter reflects the state of exile (vv. 3, 5), with no resting place (v. 3), no one coming to her festivals (v. 4) and a state of desolation (vv. 4, 13). Personified Jerusalem in this passage has nowhere to turn. In the cultural context of this passage, a widow left alone would be the object of pity. The type of woman described in this passage experiences great shame. She is destitute and forlorn. Even as she turns to others for help, there is no one to comfort her. This story is left unresolved. The shame and loneliness experienced by the suffering city seems to have no recourse. The lament acknowledges the reality of the situation. Implied in this pathetic reality, however, is hope: YHWH and no one else will be the source of help.

The absence of a human and worldly comforter compels Jerusalem to turn to God. When dealing with a painful and shameful history, the absence of an outside comforter may be a positive development. In the book of Job, we encounter Job's friends who offer seemingly inappropriate and irrelevant "comfort." Their commentary is unwelcomed and unhelpful. Their most effective support could be summarized as their willingness to sit with their suffering friend. The acknowledgment that there is no human wisdom that can be offered may be our best offering to the suffering other.

In recent years, there have been a number of cases where black youth were killed and the gunmen were acquitted of murder charges. An appropriate and deep sense of distress emerged from many in the African American community, raising questions about the "worth" of young black men in American society. The lament of many African Americans reflects a deep-seated, long-standing, historic suffering experienced by their community. Often, Facebook and Twitter provide the public outlets for this national lament over the devaluing of young black men whose lives are deemed unworthy of justice. As I've scrolled through the lament offered on social media, I've grown increasingly distressed about the type of comments offered by some whites—often white Christians—who want to argue the details of the law and analyze the issues on legal merits. They want to dismiss the racialized components of the issues, and they interrupt the lament in inappropriate ways.

The example in Lamentations (as well as the book of Job) may be that lament needs to run its course. Neither the absence of human comfort nor the human attempt to diffuse and minimize the emotional response of lament serves the suffering other. It only adds to the suffering. The appropriate response would be to express presence and an expression of lament alongside the sufferer rather than explain away the suffering. Xuan Huong Thi Pham points out that one of the key expressions of Lamentations is that it "laments the humanly impossible task of comforting in the face of such tragic circumstances."[25] The inability to offer comfort should compel us to acknowledge our total inability and turn to God for the answers.

Lament presents the opportunity to call out to God for his mercy. It acknowledges the need for God's justice and mercy that does not arise out of one's own strength and ability. Lament challenges the church to acknowledge real suffering and plead with God for his intervention. The book of Lamentations raises an important question about the value of persistent lament. The evangelical culture moves too quickly to praise from lament. We do not hear from all of the voices in the North American evangelical context. Instead, we opt for quick and easy answers to complex issues. We want to move on to the happier message of success and triumph and cover up the message of those who suffer.

My late friend Richard Twiss told me a story of his time at an international gathering of evangelicals. He was the only Native American from the United States, so when it came time for delegates to share their experiences, Richard boldly shared how the Native American voice had been left out of the American evangelical story. But before he could finish his comment, the moderator of the meeting stated that in the interest of time they needed to move on quickly to other matters, which turned out to be stories about the great successes that Americans were experiencing in overseas missionary efforts.

The crying out to God in lament over a broken history is often set aside in favor of a triumphalistic narrative. We are too busy patting ourselves on the back over the problem-solving abilities of the triumphant American church to cry out to God in lament. But lament cannot and must not be ignored. In the biblical world, hope does not emerge from the self-aggrandizing act of recounting our successes. It is the desperate plea for God's intervention that arises out of lament that reveals a flickering glimpse of hope. What about us? Even after tasting God's fury and wrath, do we still have hope?

Do we still have the ability to worship even as our faith is being tested? Or do we rush to praise, even in the absence of lament?

For the complete biblical narrative to take root in our community, lament has to become a part of our story. Emmanuel Katongole emphasizes that "any resurrection of the church as the body of Christ must begin with lament, which is an honest look at the brokenness of the church. Without lament, we move on too quickly to reconstruction."[26] Lament calls us to examine the work of reconciliation between those who live under suffering with those who live in celebration. Lamentations challenges our celebratory assumptions with the reality of suffering.

Lamentations 2

The plenary speaker's voice resounded throughout the large church sanctuary. Nearly four thousand participants convened for one of the largest evangelical pastor's conferences in North America. Current and future church pastors gathered to hear from inspirational Christian leaders. The plenary speaker that strode the platform that afternoon was one of the most prominent evangelical pastors in the last twenty years. However, the content of his presentation left much to be desired.

During the speech (I hesitate to use the term *sermon* for what he presented that day), the pastor repeated the mantra: "The sky's the limit . . . so reach for the stars." Scriptural references never surfaced. An abstract platitude replaced any reference to Jesus. The phrases employed by the speaker could have been offered by a motivational speaker at the local airport Comfort Inn. Vague but tweetable platitudes meant that a church planter in the audience could apply these empty words in any way deemed relevant.

Maybe even more disturbing than the theologically vacuous plenary session was the persistent theme of striving for success and moving toward the victory of the American church. Throughout the conference, the attendees repeatedly encountered the theme of triumphalism and exceptionalism. The American church would succeed in conquering the problem of church decline. The American church would triumph over the challenges of postmodernism. Any practical, applicable and workable methods would be employed to ensure the great accomplishment of the evangelical church in the United States.

A triumphant and success-oriented narrative limits the twenty-first-century American evangelical theological imagination. The narrative of triumph silences a narrative of suffering. But the book of Lamentations offers a counternarrative to the predominant narrative of the American evangelical church. Lamentations highlights the importance of the lament of a suffering community. In Lamentations 2, we encounter a suffering community coming to terms with their narrative. They embrace the necessary work of God in the place of suffering rather than quickly jumping to the easy answers.

Lamentations 2 suggests a proper response to God's sovereignty. The narrative of suffering and the lament that accompanies suffering is evidenced in Lamentations 2 as God's people move toward an acknowledgment of who is in charge. In the humility necessary to acknowledge their shortcomings, the survivors of the destruction of Jerusalem can respond appropriately to God's judgment. The dismantling of privilege requires the disavowal of any pretense of exceptionalism. Lamentations 2 offers a possibility of the expansion of the American evangelical theological imagination in order to encompass suffering and lament, which a privileged perspective may not allow. Lamentations calls us to embrace a narrative of suffering in order to understand the fullness of God's message for his people.

God Is Faithful

Lamentations 2:1-8

A pastor struggles with the right words to say to the family of a child in a neonatal intensive-care unit. A community activist grapples with the reality of actions by the government that will cut support for the neediest in her community. A youth pastor recoils at the thought of attending yet another funeral of one of his youth who was a victim of violence. What would happen to our faith if we believed that God reigns sovereign over both our celebration *and* our suffering?

In Lamentations 1, we heard the lament over Jerusalem by the city's survivors. The very real pain of the suffering people is heard. The main subject of Lamentations 1 is the voices of the suffering. In the second chapter of Lamentations, God emerges as the main subject. In verses 1-8, all of the actions against Jerusalem are attributed to God:

> the Lord has covered . . . he has hurled down . . . the Lord has swallowed up . . . he has torn down . . . he has cut off every horn . . . he has withdrawn his right hand . . . he has strung his bow . . . he has slain . . . he has poured out his wrath . . . he has swallowed up . . . he has multiplied mourning and lamen-

tation . . . he has laid waste . . . he has destroyed . . . he has
spurned . . . the Lord has rejected . . . he has given the walls of
her palaces into the hands of the enemy . . . the Lord determined to tear down the wall.

Every single line in Lamentations 2:1-8 places God as the subject
followed by a corresponding action.

God is the main actor in Lamentations 2. While the marauders
from the North may be the human agents of destruction, Leslie
Allen points out that in Lamentations 2, these human enemies "are
blatantly replaced by Yahweh, whose instruments the troops were
deemed to be, just as Assyria was 'the rod of' Yahweh's 'anger' against
Judah in Isaiah 10:5. Confronted by such a coalition of enemies, Judah's military forces stood no chance."[1] Lamentations 2 emphasizes
God's role in the fall of Jerusalem. YHWH used Israel's enemies to
bring judgment upon Jerusalem. With God as the primary subject,
the suffering of Jerusalem is not beyond the boundaries of his
purview because nothing exists outside of his sovereignty.

In the book of Lamentations, God's people are faced with a difficult truth. What if God proves to be the *source* of suffering? What
if the humiliation and degradation experienced during the destruction of Jerusalem is God's will? Could lament simply express
a weak "amen" of a powerless people to God's actions? We are reminded at this point that Israel has a history of rebellion against
God. God's actions are not capricious, but instead his actions reveal
a constancy and integrity of character and ultimate faithfulness to
his own words and to the covenant.

Second Kings 25:8-21 describes the devastation of Jerusalem. Nebuchadnezzar's commander Nebuzaradan led the conquest of Jerusalem. "He set fire to the temple of the LORD, the royal palace and all
the houses of Jerusalem. Every important building he burned down"
(v. 9). They "broke down the walls around Jerusalem. . . . [And] carried

into exile the people who remained in the city" (vv. 10, 11). The passage continues with a description of the pillaging of the temple and the names of key leaders taken away into exile or executed. "So Judah went into captivity, away from her land" (v. 21). The destruction described in 2 Kings 25 traces back to the covenant curses promised in Deuteronomy 28.

Deuteronomy 28 initially begins with promises of blessing for Israel for obedience, but shifts toward the negative consequences of disobedience in verse 15: "However, if you do not obey the LORD your God and do not carefully follow all his commands and decrees I am giving you today, all these curses will come on you and overtake you" (v. 15); "You will be cursed in the city" (v. 16); "The LORD will cause you to be defeated before your enemies" (v. 25); "The LORD will drive you and the king you set over you to a nation unknown to you or your ancestors" (v. 36); "The LORD will bring a nation against you from far away, from the ends of the earth, like an eagle swooping down, a nation whose language you will not understand" (v. 49); "They will lay siege to all the cities throughout your land until the high fortified walls in which you trust fall down" (v. 52); "You will be uprooted from the land you are entering to possess. Then the LORD will scatter you among all nations, from one end of the earth to the other" (vv. 63-64). In the exhaustive list of curses found in the book of Deuteronomy, one of the most significant curses was exile. The description of the fall of Jerusalem in 2 Kings 25 fulfills the prophetic curses warned of in Deuteronomy. The loss of their homeland would mean that Israel's precious inheritance had been taken away.

GOD'S FIDELITY TO HIS CHARACTER

Jerusalem's fall has notable spiritual significance. To the people of Israel, Jerusalem had symbolized Israel's unique relationship with YHWH. The loss of Jerusalem is the culmination of the curses promised in the book of Deuteronomy. From the perspective of God's people, the fall of Jerusalem and Israel's exile could lead to a loss of confidence in God. The assurance that God would always be there for them is now called into question. Yet this judgment is justified. In fact, it is actually a fulfillment of God's promises, revealing his faithfulness. YHWH's integrity in enacting proper judgment should lead to the recognition that his integrity will *also* be evidenced in the process of restoration.

The destruction of Jerusalem reveals YHWH's fidelity to the covenant curses, which reflects his fidelity to the covenant itself. If God stays true to his character, he *has* to judge unrighteousness and injustice because he takes sin seriously. And because God is faithful in bringing judgment upon Israel's disobedience, there is also certainty to God's redemption. God is true to his word in fulfilling the covenant curses, and therefore he will also be faithful in fulfilling the covenant blessings.

It is appropriate for the lamenter to experience a level of *dis*ease and *dis*comfort with the harsh judgment imposed upon Jerusalem. However, lament also acknowledges God's right to judge humanity. God abhors sin, therefore the prophet should also abhor sin. The prophetic role is to point out and call out sin, not just in the individual context but also in the corporate context. The faithfulness to point out sin is also an implicit faithfulness in God's desire to restore. He has judged rightly and he will restore rightly. Are we willing, therefore, to accept God's righteous and appropriate judgment?

Revelation 18 reveals glimpses of the ultimate judgment of God. The angel declares that impure and unclean Babylon has fallen. When it falls, we are told that "the nations have drunk the maddening wine of her adulteries. / The kings of the earth committed adultery with her, / and the merchants of the earth grew rich from her excessive luxuries" (v. 3). Righteous judgment has fallen on Babylon. Rather than rejoicing in God's righteous judgment, there is weeping and mourning over the fall of Babylon. Too much had been invested in the systems of Babylon. God's righteous judgment falls on the nations because the people have prostituted themselves with Babylon.

J. Richard Middleton and Brian J. Walsh assert that the fall of modernity can be compared to the fall of Babylon in the book of Revelation. Middleton and Walsh describe the onset of postmodernity alongside the collapse of modernity. They see new possibilities in the changes that are occurring. "The collapse of the tower of modernity is good news. Postmodernity opens up genuine new possibilities for human cultural formation and should be welcomed as a positive historical opportunity."[2] Whatever our view of postmodernity, we must acknowledge that many significant changes have occurred in the previous century. The collapse of the old order of modernity may be the right event at the right time. However, like the nations that have grown rich from Babylon, how much has American Christianity grown rich from the systems that elevated Western expressions of modernity?

Lament presents an appropriate response to suffering, but lament must also correspond to the recognition that God is in control. The expression of God as the main subject of agency in Lamentations 2 reveals a God who is indeed sovereign over history and serves as the righteous judge over history. If we trust in God's sovereignty to judge, then we can also hope in God's sovereignty to expand his reign over human history. Lamentations 2 asserts that God is the primary actor in Jerusalem's history. The acknowledgment of this sovereignty should free those of us who put our trust in God to not put ourselves in the place of God. We are called not to fix everyone else's problems, but to acknowledge our place as those who live under God's authority. Lamentations 2, therefore, calls us to suffer alongside those who suffer (such as those who have fallen away from faith or those who have been hurt by the systems of Christianity that have oppressed the marginalized). Lamentations 2 calls us to recognize God's faithfulness to judge unrighteous and oppressive systems.

An important aspect of Lamentations is the challenge to accept historical reality and to embrace God's sovereignty over history. We are called to lament over suffering and pain, but also to recognize God's larger work. Part of our discomfort with Lamentations is the sense that suffering may be an appropriate reality given our words and our deeds. Have we behaved inappropriately as a church endowed with great affluence? Have we sinned against God in squandering our many blessings? Instead of investing in the kingdom of God on a global scale, have we invested in the fallen systems of Western culture and her political and economic systems? Are we so invested in the Western cultural captivity of the church that we are unable to accept God's right judgment on the broken system of oppression? The Western church elevates values of Western culture, even at the expense of biblical values. Western cultural values and how we live out Christian faith in the United States are presented as theologically normative and oppress voices from outside of the Western context.[3]

In the twenty-first century, we are witness to the last throes of the Western cultural captivity of the American church. The demographic realities of twenty-first-century Christianity need to be acknowledged as the closing of a chapter of church history. At the beginning of the twentieth century, the overwhelming majority of the world's Christian population resided in Europe and North America. At the beginning of the twenty-first century, the clear majority of the world's Christian population resides in Africa, Asia and Latin America.[4] The population dominance of Western Christianity has already come to an end. Western cultural captivity and dominance as an epoch of church history is also coming to an end. But as Western Christians wring their hands over the implosion of modern, Enlightenment Christianity and the subsequent decline of European and Euro-American Christianity, is it more appropriate to acknowledge the justness of God's sovereign judgment of unjust systems? Should we embrace this moment as God's sovereign will?

Lamentations 2 reminds us that God is faithful to his covenant. His work of judgment and restoration are at his mercy and will. He is the subject with the agency to act in history, so the changing shape of world Christianity in the twenty-first century reflects God's sovereign will. While we may lament the loss we experience in Western Christianity, we should acknowledge that it may be God's will that oppressive Western systems decline.

Several years ago, I presented a plenary session on the growing diversity of American Christianity at a pastor's conference. I presented on the reality of the decline of Western Christianity and the dynamic rise of non-Western Christianity, even in the United States. I presented this information through the use of statistics that showed that European and Euro-American Christianity was in significant decline. In the middle of this presentation, a prominent white evangelical leader who was one of the organizers of the conference made quite a display in walking out of the plenary session from a middle seat in the front row of the auditorium.

A few weeks later, this evangelical leader called me to say that he thought it was inappropriate of me to present the decline of Western Christianity. He felt that I had overemphasized the rise of non-Western Christianity and was diminishing the role of the American church. This evangelical leader was emotionally unprepared to face the reality of a Western (and maybe more significantly, American) Christianity on the decline. More than that, his words indicated to me an insecurity; I did not hear the desire to rejoice in the good work that God was doing in the increasing diversity of Christianity around the world. Instead, he insisted on extolling the virtues and worth of American Christianity, a system he had invested in heavily.

American Christians may be fearful of the dramatic changes that have already occurred in the world and in American Christianity. Could that fear be rooted in a loss of power as the demographics of world Christianity begin to favor non-Western nations? But these changes in Christianity may be exactly what God intended, requiring American Christians to relinquish a historical dominance and embrace a greater mutuality, equality and reciprocity in twenty-first-century world Christianity.

If we are to accept the appropriateness of God's judgment, then the fall of the Western cultural captivity of Christianity should be seen as the end of a life cycle for a particular theological frame of reference in a particular era of Christian history—an era that has lamentably drawn to an end. In the twenty-first century, American Christians may be called to acknowledge God's sovereign move in bringing spiritual renewal and revival to the majority world, while the European and Euro-American churches continue their decline.

Lamentations 2:1-8 reminds us that God's sovereignty in judgment also directs us toward God's sovereignty in restoration. The church, therefore, acknowledges the appropriate end of the era of Western Christian dominance and seeks God's sovereign covenant loyalty to preserve his people through the preservation of his church through non-Western forms of Christianity. If we trust that God's covenant loyalty to the church is predicated upon his will and not our own, we should be more willing to embrace what God is doing in the global expression of Christianity. Instead of desperately clinging to Western forms of evangelicalism, we could learn from God's sustaining work evident in global Pentecostalism and non-Western theologies. Our conversations as a church would shift from preventing the decline of middle-class, white evangelicalism to embracing the rise of world Christianity. Lamentations calls us to reflect on God's judgment and return the focus back to God. God remains the only source of present and future hope, even as he stands as the righteous source of judgment.

LAMENT OVER A CITY

Lamentations 2:1-9

Lamentations does not fit neatly into the pre-existing categories of a lament psalm. The book of Lamentations exhibits a wide range of subgenres within the larger genre of lament. We have already discussed the use of the funeral dirge as one of the genres employed throughout the book in chapters 1, 2 and 4. One of the unique elements of the book of Lamentations is that it also follows the format of a "lament over the fallen city,"[1] or the city-lament genre. The city lament was found frequently in the context of the ancient Near East, with the "Lamentation over the Destruction of Ur" and "The Lamentation over the Destruction of Sumer and Ur"[2] presenting examples of this genre from ancient Mesopotamia. F. W. Dobbs-Allsopp notes that "a comparison of the generic repertoire of the Mesopotamian city laments with Lamentations reveals no less than nine important features held in common."[3] The nine features are "subject and mood, structure and poetic technique, divine abandonment, assignment of responsibility, divine agent of destruction, destruction, weeping goddess, lamentation, and restoration of the city and return of the gods."[4]

The use of the city-lament genre is evident throughout the entire book, but we can recognize some key features of the city lament in Lamentations 2. The object of lament is the city of Jerusalem, also referenced as the "Daughter of Zion" (vv. 1, 4, 8, 10). The city is portrayed as abandoned by God (vv. 3, 7) and it is God who is the agent of the city's destruction (vv. 2, 5, 6, 8, 9). The weeping goddess in the Mesopotamian city laments is replaced by the mourning and lamentation of a feminine personified Jerusalem (v. 5).[5] In Lamentations 2, the city of Jerusalem functions as both the victim and the object of pity and lament.

Jerusalem fell victim to the "Day of the Lord." Dobbs-Allsopp notes that

> much of the imagery [in Lamentations 2:1-8] is drawn from the ancient Israelite prophetic traditions about the "Day of the Lord." These traditions assert the belief that God will intervene in history and defeat God's and Israel's enemies in battle. They feature most prominently depictions of battle imagery, God envisioned as warrior, divine anger, fire and darkness and gloom.[6]

Jerusalem's suffering is amplified by the humiliation of God's judgment falling upon a people who saw this type of judgment as reserved for their enemies.

Lamentations 2 vividly describes Jerusalem's destruction from every angle, listing all of the key spiritual and physical features of Jerusalem. The city has lost her spiritual vitality as YHWH's "place of meeting" has been destroyed. Spiritual worship life exemplified by "her appointed festivals and her Sabbaths" (v. 6), the "altar" and "sanctuary" (v. 7) are no more. The loss of worship also destroys the patterns and rhythms of life that once brought order and stability. The architecture and physical structures of the city—"palaces" and "strongholds" (v. 5), "the wall" and "ramparts" (v. 8), and "gates" and "bars" that keep out the enemy (v. 9)—have been laid waste. The leaders of the city, "both king and priest" (v. 6), as well as the prophets and the elders (vv. 9, 10) have been exiled. Every aspect of civic and religious life in the city of Jerusalem has been disrupted, requiring a lament over the fallen city. Similar to the use of the funeral dirge, the city lament calls the people to deal with the reality of the situation: the city has fallen.

In employing the city-lament genre, Lamentations borrows a familiar ancient Near Eastern form to express the depth of sorrow that is experienced by both the community and the individuals in the community. The genre of the Mesopotamian city lament requires an accurate depiction of the history of the fallen city before it looks toward a new future. In the ancient world, these city laments "were performed as a part of the cultic ceremonies in which the foundations of the old sanctuaries were razed, just prior to the initiation of any restoration work. . . . The classic city laments typically close by celebrating the return of the gods and depicting the restoration of the city and temples."[7] However, the use of the city lament in Lamentations presents a slightly different intention from other city laments. Dobbs-Allsopp notes that "the motifs of the return of the gods and the restoration of the temples and city, integral to the Mesopotamian city laments, are completely absent in Lamentations."[8] The Mesopotamian city laments, therefore, assume an imminent celebration as the gods return to a restored city. Lamentations holds no such promise. Instead, the priority of Lamentations is to offer a mourning that embraces the reality of suffering.

Lamentations does not explicitly state the future hope of restoration of life as usual for Jerusalem. Instead, Lamentations probably served "as the kinds of public mourning ceremonies that presumably took place at the site of the destroyed city throughout the exilic period to commemorate the catastrophe."[9] In current expressions of Judaism, Lamentations is read during the Tisha B'Av ceremony. The liturgy of Tisha B'Av not only includes the book of

Lamentations but also a recounting of the stories of suffering and tragedy throughout the history of Judaism, including the Holocaust. Lamentations speaks of a tragic event so its commemoration includes the subsequent tragedies that have been witnessed by the city of Jerusalem and by the Jewish people. Lamentations as a city lament calls for an accurate picture of the fallen city without necessarily ensuring an optimistic future. Lamentations 2 fulfills the city-lament genre with a realistic depiction of the pain and destruction experienced by Jerusalem.

The city lament draws YHWH's attention to the very real suffering of the city. Lamentations speaks to a present reality rather than a future dream or a symbolic abstraction. Lamentations as a city lament follows the features of an ancient Near Eastern city lament in detailing the comprehensive destruction of the city. Much like the funeral dirge, those who lament the destruction of the city are forced to deal with the reality of suffering. The city lament is not an occasion to dream of a better future for the city, it is a time to recognize the concrete and material realities of the city. So the city lament as expressed in Lamentations does not deal with hypotheticals or abstract ideals, it deals with the destroyed city that smolders before them.

The city lament also places the city at the center of the narrative. The first two chapters of Lamentations employ the literary device of the personification of the city of Jerusalem to narrow the focus of the lament. The emotional weight of suffering is amplified and highlighted by the personification of Jerusalem as Daughter Zion. Suffering is not abstract but real because it happens to a real being: a personified Jerusalem who suffers under the judgment of YHWH. Thus the acts of YHWH against the city are felt in human terms.

The city experiences suffering together rather than in isolation. As the city is personified, the remnant of Jerusalem suffers corporately, revealing a depth of pain at the hand of God. Personification does not allow for an explaining away of suffering. Personification of Jerusalem in Lamentations and the city lament that addresses the personified city does not deal with an abstract concept. The goal of the city lament is to bring attention to a very real situation being experienced collectively by the remnant of Jerusalem. It does not allow the remnant to romanticize the city or to abstract the city in order to exhibit control. The city is a major character in the process of lament and cannot be dismissed as simply an object of manipulation by those who remain.

Ministry in the city can often focus on symbolic ideals. We may idealize and even romanticize the city beyond its material reality. Instead of lamenting the actual situation of the city as demanded by the city-lament genre as employed in the book of Lamentations, we may long for an idealized future for our city. In urban ministry, there is a strong tendency toward an image of what the city should be. Often, that image may reflect the image of a successful suburban ministry and assumptions about a flourishing life in a gentrified urban neighborhood. A city lament brings the story of the city to its actual material setting and reality. The city is not an object to be fixed or manipulated—it is the concrete reality of lives and souls that live in the city.

Lamentations deals with the city on real terms. A funeral dirge is offered because the city has died. The city is described in real, concrete terms. Jerusalem is mourned not because it is an abstract ideal, but because it is home to God's people. The mourning that is offered by the residents of Jerusalem is deeply felt because it arises out of the very real experience of trauma and suffering.

In Western society, the city is often portrayed in abstract, philosophical terms.[10] Christianity in the West focuses on the concept of the city not as the actual gathering of people within a geographic boundary but as the symbolic locus of human activity. For example, Augustine used the term to represent a particular state of human existence. The city of man and the city of God do not refer to geographic boundaries but instead speak to a higher concept or ideal.

The city of God is the realm of God's dominion and authority. The earthly city is the work of human hands.[11] Augustine's development of a contrasting framework between God's city and the human city furthers the abstract understanding of the city. More than a location, the city serves as a summary of human life or the transcendent work of God outside of the realm of the flesh.

In recent years, the abstraction of the city continues through American Christians who do not necessarily live in the city. The city comes to symbolize the collection of humanity that can yield either a positive, virtuous end or a negative, destructive end. The treatment of the city as an abstract ideal (usually conflated with the idea of secular society) leads to idealizing the city as a "mission field." The city-lament genre of Lamentations calls for an honest engagement with the city. Like the funeral-dirge genre of Lamentations, the city-lament genre deals with reality. Lamentations as a city lament contrasts to the idealization of the city in contemporary Christianity. The portrayal of the city in extreme abstract categories of all good or all bad leads to a dysfunctional engagement with the city.

American Christianity's relationship to the city yields a complex and shifting narrative. In the early stages of American church history, Christians held an optimistic view of the future of the American continent and American cities. The first governor of Massachusetts, John Winthrop, believed that America "was to be 'a city set on a hill' . . . God's country with a mission to perform."[12] William Clebsch notes "the vision of the new world as locus for a new city. . . . The new world prompted Christians from the sixteenth century through the nineteenth to think of America as the last and best of human societies following the westward course of empire."[13] Colonial American Christians anticipated that the cities of the New World would become new Jerusalems and Zions.

This optimistic view of the American city shifts over the course of the nineteenth and twentieth century. The many decades between the end of the Civil War and the end of the Second World War witnessed drastic changes in the landscape of the city. The migration of African Americans from former slave states coupled with the influx of non-Protestant and non-Western European immigrants into the North and East coast resulted in the notable growth of these cities.

The influx of these "unwanted elements" in the cities, however, meant that whites, who had previously seen the American cities as places of great hope and promise, now saw them as dangerous places. Robert Orsi analyzes that

> in the feverish imaginations of antebellum anti-Catholic literary provocateurs, city neighborhoods appeared as caves of rum and Romanism, mysterious and forbidding, a threat to democracy, Protestantism, and virtue alike. Journalism, anti-Catholic and anti-immigrant polemics, temperance pamphlets, and evangelical tracts together created a luridly compelling anti-urban genre that depicted the city as the vicious destroyer of the common good, of family life and individual character, and counter-posed the city to an idealized image of small-town life.[14]

Meanwhile, the suburban communities offered an attractive alternative for former residents of the city. Amanda Seligman notes that "in the years after World War II, a modern form of suburb, fostered by new tools, opened up around the country. Innovative financing techniques, subsidized by the federal government, enabled millions of white Americans to purchase property beyond city limits."[15]

The result of this shifting perspective was white flight. The twentieth century, therefore, witnessed the departure of whites and white churches from the city in significant numbers. In *The Warmth of Other Suns*, Isabel Wilkerson notes:

> After World War II, Chicago, Detroit, Cleveland, and other northern and western cities would witness a fitful migration

of whites out of their urban strongholds. The far-out precincts and the inner-ring suburbs became sanctuaries for battle-weary whites seeking, with government incentives, to replicate the havens they once had in the cities.[16]

The suburbs became the new outposts for white Christians fearful of the changes in the city. Twentieth-century Christians, therefore, adopted a strong sense of distinction and separation between the city and noncity regions. This demarcation led to the perception of the modern city as all that is wrong with the world, while the suburbs could be seen as what is right with the world. The suburbs have become the New Jerusalem with the cities now relegated as Babylon.[17] In contrast to the historical context of Lamentations where the remnant lament the destruction of the city, many white evangelicals abandoned the city in droves in the twentieth century and now offer a postmortem of the city from afar.

The city is a gathering of people in a specific location that expresses the vast range of human life and activity in that location. It is the neighborhood where people come together. This gathering of human life in the city raises the same sense of need as any gathering. In this way, it reflects the power of community life. It is not, however, an abstract reality only to be seen through its metaphorical usage.

If the city is merely an abstraction, then the response to that abstraction is another abstraction. Urban theology can deteriorate into an abstract theology confronting an abstract concept. The path to change is further philosophical and theological abstraction and the triumph of ideas and values over any real on-the-ground change. So urban ministry merely becomes the battle of ideas and principles. This approach can reduce our understanding of the city to an oversimplification, categorizing it in all good or all bad terms.

Seeing injustice in the city through an abstracted lens allows the individual to disassociate from the reality of injustice. Injustice can be objectified and depersonalized. Hunger, homelessness and racism are very real injustices, but they can be misunderstood when taken in an abstracted form. One of the most effective means of disengaging the church from the work of justice is making injustice a philosophical concept.

With this high level of abstraction, it is easy to scapegoat individuals and move responsibility to the other rather than admit personal responsibility. When a mass shooting of children at a school occurs, we will claim that this horrible action is the result of just one crazed gunman rather than consider the possibility of a social-structure problem at work. Some will argue that it does no good to consider social action when clearly this action can be blamed in its totality on just one individual. But we do not consider that doing nothing to prevent future tragedies in the face of a national tragedy demonstrates the sin of omission.

We practice this same abstract thinking in our relation with the rest of the world. We write checks to end human trafficking but lack concern for how our demand for cheap, disposable clothing generates a larger system of exploitation. We forget that hunger in Africa has any connection to the history of Western colonialism from which we in the West have significantly benefited. We are oblivious to the need for corporate responsibility to address colonial abuses in the previous centuries. We are able to abstract our justice efforts from the material reality of the history of injustice in the relationship between the Western colonizers and the colonized who still suffer the ill effects of a colonial history.

We abstract injustice, allowing ourselves to believe we no longer have a direct hand in it. We make injustice impersonal; if everyone is responsible, then no one is responsible. But justice should not be abstracted to a corporate concept that justifies ongoing individual injustice. Justice is social *and* corporate, but it requires a personal face.

If the city is an actual location, neighborhood and community, urban ministry should draw from a theology that has a concrete expression. The church in the city is not merely engaging in a metaphorical battle in the spiritual realm, but it is working to bring real change to a material reality. The movement away from the city as an abstraction results in the possibility that the presence of the church shaped by Christian theology could have an impact on the human city. The actual, physical realm of the city provides a place for concrete action by the church.

The city lament employed in the book of Lamentations follows the general pattern of city laments of Mesopotamia, drawing attention to the devastation enacted upon the city. Both use personification to deal with the very human nature of the suffering endured by the residents of a devastated city. But Lamentations diverges from the Mesopotamian city lament when it focuses on the sins of the residents rather than the capricious nature of the gods to bring judgment. Instead, Lamentations offers a true depiction of the sins of the city and the subsequent judgment. It does not move quickly beyond the human experience to find an easy answer from outside the city.

The book of Lamentations does not dabble in an abstract depiction of the city. It involves the whole spectrum of city life, including the role of Jerusalem in the spiritual realm and the destruction of the city in the physical realm. The city in Lamentations is not merely an abstract concept that references politics or culture. Through our reading of Lamentations, we view the city not only for what it represents, but for what the city actually is, even if that is a fallen city requiring lament. By abstracting and spiritualizing the city, we view the city as a problem to be solved with abstract ideas and concepts. The city lament reminds us that life in the city is not to be abstracted, but instead, it is to be understood through the lens of real-life experiences and the stories of those who actually live there.

Privilege and Exceptionalism

Lamentations 2:6-9

The fall of Jerusalem is particularly disturbing to the residents who held a high view of their own worth as a city. Jerusalem was David's city. The Psalms attest to the unique place of Jerusalem in the world. "I have installed my king on Zion, my holy mountain" (Ps 2:6); "The name of the LORD will be declared in Zion and his praise in Jerusalem" (Ps 102:21); and "Praise be to the LORD from Zion, to him who dwells in Jerusalem" (Ps 135:21) provide a sample of Israel's self-portrayal of Jerusalem as an exceptional place suitable for the presence of YHWH.

Jerusalem was home to the temple of the Lord. It was the place of affirmation that Israel had a unique covenantal relationship with YHWH. "The destruction of Jerusalem, the loss of statehood, the deportation of the leaders and the cessation of cultic religion were epochal events for they marked the end of one era and the beginning of another."[1] The destruction of Jerusalem represents a comprehensive disaster that challenged the self-perception of God's people. It was "an event without precedent in the history of Israel, and it would become a turning point in Jewish religious development."[2]

In Lamentations 1, we begin to see the response to this national tragedy with bitter weeping (v. 2) and the acknowledgment that all the majesty, splendor and valuable treasures have been taken away (vv. 6-7). The holiness of Jerusalem has now been debased into filth, shame and nakedness (v. 8). The great pride in Jerusalem as the center of worship is replaced with mourning over the cessation of worship (v. 4).

Lamentations 2 continues to assert this great sense of loss over the city of Jerusalem. The current sorry state of Jerusalem is contrasted by her former glory. Narrated for us is the systematic dismantling of Jerusalem and how that dismantling reveals the underlying perception of exceptionalism by the citizens of Jerusalem. Adele Berlin notes that

> the language in vv. 1-10 projects a feeling of strength and power
> in two ways. First, it employs many verbs signifying strong and
> violent action: hurled down, consumed, chopped off, destroyed,
> demolished, wrecked. It is with brute force that God has acted.
> Second, it describes in detail the fortifications of the city—its
> walls, citadels, strongholds, ramparts and gates.[3]

The force needed to overcome the city reveals the perception of Jerusalem as a once-powerful city. It required the full force of YHWH's power to demolish it.

The depth to which Jerusalem has fallen is emphasized by the heights it once occupied. Lamentations 2:1-9 narrates the theological significance of the fall of Jerusalem to God's people. Jerusalem has been hurled from heaven to earth (v. 1) and its horn (strength) has been cut off (v. 3). Jerusalem has become an enemy to YHWH, who poured out his wrath like fire (v. 4). This description reveals the great sense of loss, and the tragedy of the fall of Jerusalem is heightened by Jerusalem's self-perception as an exceptional and special city.

Starting with verse 6, we begin to see Jerusalem's self-perception based upon their unique position as the gathering place for YHWH worship. Jerusalem naively believed that their status as the keepers of the temple meant that no judgment would befall them. The temple of YHWH was their protection. Surely God would never judge his chosen people and his very own temple of worship. But verse 9 reveals that Jerusalem has lost what made it unique: "The law is no more." Jerusalem's uniqueness was not based upon its own merit but on God's grace—the grace that gave his Word to his people and the privilege of offering him worship. All of these privileges flowed from God's presence. Lamentations 2:7 reveals that "the Lord has rejected his altar and abandoned his sanctuary." Since YHWH's presence determined Jerusalem's standing as the center for worship, his departure signals that they are no longer the center of YHWH worship. Their privilege had been revoked.

This loss of privilege is not only experienced by Jerusalem, it is also acknowledged by other nations, heightening Jerusalem's shame. Lamentations 2:15 reveals that "All who pass your way clap their hands at you; / they scoff and shake their heads at Daughter Jerusalem: / 'Is this the city that was called / the perfection of beauty, / the joy of the whole earth?'" The sarcastic comment by those who pass by reveals how far Jerusalem has fallen. Lament is a response to this fall, and an important ingredient in the ability to lament is the ability to recognize the role of privilege. The people of God made significant assumptions about their privileged position. They assumed a level of protection that arose from their sense of exceptionalism and privilege. Lamentations reminds us that privilege needs to be acknowledged but cannot be assumed.

Lamentations reveals the tendency of a sinful people to have an elevated view of themselves. Prior to the city's destruction, the residents of Jerusalem viewed themselves as an exceptional and privileged people. In American Christianity, the same tendency toward privilege also exists. There is an underlying belief that American Christians have been the standard-bearers of Christianity for several centuries. There is a sense of being the exceptional church, resulting in the missionary endeavor and vision. This favored church status has led to a belief in a favored nation status. But this sense of American exceptionalism and even the sense of exceptionalism for the American church cannot be justified through Scripture.

Sadly, American exceptionalism and the idea of God's unique blessing upon the United States has become a common statement by American Christians. During the 2012 presidential elections, Governor Mitt Romney closed out the debate on foreign policy with the statement: "America is the hope of the world." Despite the theological problem of replacing Jesus with the United States, I was surprised by the number of evangelical Christians who supported this statement. American Christians are just as susceptible to being caught up in American exceptionalism as the rest of American society. Some who read the sentences above may assume that I am anti-American and even anti-Christian for questioning American exceptionalism, but American exceptionalism finds no support in the Scriptures. In fact, Lamentations reveals that exceptionalism is a pronouncement by God and characterized by God's gracious presence. To believe that the United States has assumed the mantle of blessing from Israel is a faulty assumption. Israel's exceptionalism arises from God's grace. There is no scriptural support that the United States has earned God's favor as an exceptional nation.

One of the problems of tying American exceptionalism to American Christianity is the belief that the American church becomes the arm of God, much like the United States viewed itself as the arsenal of democracy in the twentieth century. In *America and Its Guns*, James Atwood points to how American exceptionalism arises from a deep theological deficiency and moves toward a dysfunctional militarism and culture of violence. Brueggemann agrees:

"At bottom is a militant notion of US exceptionalism, that the US is peculiarly the land of freedom and bravery that must be defended at all costs. It calls forth raw exhibits of power, sometimes in the service of colonial expansionism, but short of that, simply the strutting claim of strength, control, and superiority."[4] American Christian exceptionalism can follow the same logic of strength, control and superiority that elevates the United States as the problem solvers of the world—sometimes by any means necessary.

In the fall of 2011, I was returning from a yearlong sabbatical. After nearly twelve months away from my office, quite an impressive stack of mail greeted me. I spent an entire morning opening and tossing out junk mail that had accumulated over the course of the past academic year, but there was one piece of mail that caught my eye. It was a nicely packaged DVD with the words, "The poor will not always be with us" emblazoned on the cover. As a seminary professor, I am always intrigued when Scripture is twisted to meet the needs of the communicator, so I opened the package.

The intent of this material was to challenge the church (specifically the American church) to attempt to end extreme poverty within this generation—an effort I have no problem supporting wholeheartedly. But the more subliminal message (particularly given the target audience of this material) was that the American church is responsible to bring about this change. The American church has the know-how and the resources to fix the problem. Poverty becomes another problem to solve using American ingenuity and gumption. This material furthers the self-perception of privilege for the American church. Our standing as the saviors of the world is assumed and not challenged. The book of Lamentations reminds us that privilege is a standing before God that should not be co-opted for the sake of furthering a self-perceived exceptionalism. The language of lament is the language of humility.

Triumphalistic Christianity that elevates its own sense of exceptionalism focuses on celebration furthering the dominant narrative of success and victory. The suffering narrative is considered inferior and should be ignored. Stories of successful church plants and growing megachurches with huge budgets are front and center in the dominant narrative of the successful American Christianity. Churches that meet the ideal of a typical American success story are the stories that are circulated throughout evangelicalism. Conferences must bring in big-name speakers, usually young, hip, white pastors, entrepreneurs and "thought leaders." These trends further perpetuate the triumphalistic narrative of white American evangelicalism.

A narrative of success propels white evangelicalism over and above other forms of American Christianity. Evangelicals often fail to embrace the important examples of the Spanish-speaking store-front church because they are considered too small, even though the faithful spirituality in the midst of suffering would blow away all of our purpose-driven lives. Korean American immigrants that meet faithfully at 5:00 a.m. every day to pray at the church before embarking on a twelve-hour work day are ignored because they speak a foreign language and speak English with an accent. The spiritual rituals of Native American Christian communities are perceived as exotic pagan practices that dabble in syncretism and are inferior to the rich tradition of a Taizé service. Non-Western expressions of Christianity, therefore, can be portrayed as inferior to the successful formula for ministry put forth by many white evangelicals in mainstream Christian culture.

An elevated view of one's self leads to the perception of other cultures through the lens of American Christian exceptionalism. Other cultures are viewed as diversions and interruptions to our regularly scheduled programming. Exotic cultural expressions will be accepted as long as we return to the normative form of worship, which oftentimes reflect the norms of the dominant culture. Lamentations reveals the folly of Jerusalem's self-perceived exceptionalism. Their belief that they were the center of worship because they were exceptional in some inherent way was debunked when the temple was destroyed. Their sense of strength and the projection of their power was torn down as their once-powerful city laid waste. Words of strength have been replaced with words of weakness. Lamentations points out to the remnant of Jerusalem the great folly of their self-perceived exceptionalism. How much greater is the folly of American Christians to assert American and American Christian exceptionalism?

In Lamentations 2:6-9, YHWH exhibits his anger toward the arrogance of Jerusalem's citizens. YHWH laid waste, destroyed (v. 6), rejected and abandoned his place of meeting (v. 7). Jerusalem considered itself an exceptional city as it served as YHWH's place of meeting for festivals and Sabbaths (v. 6), as well as the place for his altar and sanctuary (v. 7). But place and events did not make Jerusalem special. Instead, it was YHWH's presence that made Jerusalem special. YHWH's destruction of worship life reveals that YHWH's presence should not be taken for granted but should be embraced with great humility. It is only by his grace that his presence is found any place on earth.

ALL OF THE VOICES
ARE HEARD

Lamentations 2:10-22

As stated in chapter 3, while not the exclusive voice of Lamentations, the unidentified narrator (whom we have asserted represents the perspective, if not the actual voice, of Jeremiah) serves as the primary voice of Lamentations. The title for the book of Lamentations in the LXX is "Wailings." Lamentations may reflect the wailing perspective of the prophet Jeremiah. From his perspective arises a deep level of compassion and empathy. The book of Jeremiah reveals a very human prophet with an honest prophetic voice. Jeremiah offers a pointed reply to God in Jeremiah 20: "You deceived me, LORD, and I was deceived; / you overpowered me and prevailed. / I am ridiculed all day long; / everyone mocks me" (v. 7); "Cursed be the day I was born! / May the day my mother bore me not be blessed! / Cursed be the man who brought my father the news" (vv. 14, 15); "Why did I ever come out of the womb / to see trouble and sorrow / and to end my days in shame?" (v. 18). Jeremiah's words reveal the depth of his emotions. He does not sugarcoat his struggles. Some might even see a depressive personality in Jeremiah, but there is an authenticity to him.

He is a prophet who speaks honestly with God and with the people. When tragedy strikes, Jeremiah voices an honest lament.

As a prophet who has no problem expressing the fullness of his emotions, Jeremiah is recognized as the weeping prophet. In Jeremiah 9:1, he cries out: "Oh, that my head were a spring of water / and my eyes a fountain of tears! / I would weep day and night / for the slain of my people." The book of Jeremiah points to the historical context of Jeremiah warning Jerusalem about the impending judgment. However, Jeremiah shifts from prophetic condemnation and warning of judgment to becoming a fellow mourner over the fallen city of Jerusalem. Jeremiah directly speaks God's truth, but just as important, Jeremiah's expression of compassion reflects God's compassion. Jeremiah's heart was broken by the things that break the heart of God.

While Jeremiah serves mainly as a third-person narrator, the inclusion of additional voices in the lament presents a unique feature of Lamentations. The unique authorship of Lamentations stretches the audience to hear a perspective beyond that of the dominant culture and voice. One argument against Jeremiah authorship is the multiplicity of voices evident in the text. The narrator's voice may reflect Jeremiah's perspective on the fall of Jerusalem, but it is evident that a spectrum of voices is heard alongside Jeremiah's perspective.

Jeremiah's point of view unifies the book of Lamentations. There is also unity in the format of the poems (see chapter 8 on the use of the acrostic formula) that indicates a single redactor of the poems. While unity is evidenced in Lamentations, the dominant voice (seemingly of Jeremiah) seems to draw from multiple voices and multiple perspectives. Multiple voices and multiple genres are needed to convey the depth of emotions after the fall of Jerusalem. Kathleen O'Connor notes that "Lamentations is a book of shifting voices. . . . We can imagine the speakers gathered in a public place; they stand up, each in turn, to tell of their particular pain and demand God's attention. Each voice embodies some aspect of the suffering that belongs to the whole community."[1] In other words, Jeremiah's voice is not the only voice that is heard in Lamentations. Instead, we are introduced to the myriad of voices expressing lament. Lamentations draws from the spectrum of Jerusalem's residents to reflect the full story of Jerusalem's fall. As Adele Berlin notes: "In order to show how far-reaching the suffering was, the poet refers to its effect on various elements of the population, for example, young and old, priest and prophet, women and children."[2]

Connected to the multiple voices found in the book of Lamentations is the voice of Daughter Zion. In Lamentations 2, Jerusalem continues to be personified in the feminine voice, but "her corporate identity begins to break up into representative members of the community."[3] Different voices of Jerusalem are identified and make their appearance. They represent a wide range of citizens of Jerusalem. Rulers ("princes," v. 2), both king and priest (v. 6), the king, princes and prophets (v. 9), elders and young women (v. 10), children and infants (v. 11), mothers and wounded children (v. 12) together represent a wide spectrum of the citizens of Jerusalem.

F. W. Dobbs-Allsopp addresses the issue of the range of individual voices emerging in the book of Lamentations:

> Suffering is rendered mostly in piecemeal fashion through a succession of abrupt and fragmented images. These focus attention at the level of the individual and particular experiences: a woman raped, a child starving, a man attacked by a lion or hunted like a bird, young boys compelled into slavery and old men abused and no longer respected, a people spurned by their God. Yet that these very concrete and specific instances of suffering have been intentionally gathered together, each strung, as it were, like individual pearls on a necklace formed by the alphabetic acrostic, ensures that they mean cumulatively as well as individually.[4]

In Lamentations 2, we hear from "the elders of Daughter Zion . . . [and] the young women of Jerusalem" (v. 10). Children and infants are heard as they cry out to their mothers (vv. 11-12). Jerusalem is once again personified as a feminine voice in verse 13.

Adele Berlin also points toward the comprehensive nature of Lamentations and how the book encompasses the range of the Jerusalem populace. "Scattered through the five chapters of Lamentations are many references to the population from which one can piece together a cross-section of the inhabitants of Jerusalem."[5] Suffering is endured by the entire community. It is a communal experience. At the same time, this community experience is not merely an abstract experience. Individuals also suffer in very real ways. In engaging the spectrum of Jerusalem's residents, Lamentations gives voice to the entire community, to those whose story has been one of celebration (the kings and rulers) and those whose story has been a history of suffering (women, widows, children). Lamentations recognizes that individual voices from the full range of citizens must be heard. Lament requires the full and honest expression of suffering; that experience must encompass the full breadth of suffering.

In contrast, American evangelical Christianity often presents only the story of the dominant culture. Often, the stories from the ethnic minority communities are not deemed worthy. For example, in seminary I was taught that the very first missionary from North America was Adoniram Judson and that the first Western missionary was William Carey of England. Actually, the first missionary from North America was George Liele, a former slave who left the American colonies for Jamaica in 1782 and began a ministry of preaching in 1783, nearly three full decades before Judson would sail to Burma from Salem, Massachusetts, in 1812 and a full decade before William Carey sailed for India from England.

THE FIRST MISSIONARY: GEORGE LIELE

George Liele was born a slave (circa 1750) in the colony of Virginia. Soon after Liele's conversion in 1773, Liele launched into his preaching career, expressing a particular concern for his fellow slaves. By 1774, Liele had extended his preaching ministry into South Carolina, gathering slaves together for what could be considered the first Negro church in America. After the Revolutionary War, the recently freed Liele fled to Jamaica to escape being re-enslaved.

George Liele arrived in Jamaica as an indentured servant, but would serve as a missionary-evangelist to the island. Liele became the first Christian "to win a significant number of slaves on the Island to Christ, and certainly, as in the case of the United States, the first to organize a church made up predominantly of negroes on the Island."[6]

Liele preached in private homes and public settings drawing crowds of slaves. In a letter written in 1791, Liele reported five hundred converts and four hundred baptisms. In 1789 Liele's congregation had organized to begin work on a house of worship, which was completed in 1793 and became known as the Windward Road Chapel, the first Baptist church on the island.

Liele achieved these successful evangelistic and church planting efforts despite opposition from a powerful constituency on the island. White slave owners feared the impact upon the slave population if the slaves were to embrace Christianity. Concern arose that "if their minds are considerably enlightened by religion, or otherwise, that it would be attended with the most dangerous consequences."[7] Liele took additional precautions not to antagonize the slave owners. He wrote: "We receive none in to the church without a few lines from their owners of their good behavior toward them, and religion."[8]

Despite Liele's numerous efforts to appease the slave owners, he still faced stiff opposition. He was charged with sedition and jailed on numerous occasions on trumped-up charges.[9] In spite of these obstacles, Liele was able to baptize new converts as well as plant and organize new churches. His evangelistic and church-planting efforts led to the establishment of the Baptist denomination on the island, with slaves, freedmen and whites joining churches started by Liele. The impact of Liele's ministry continues to this day; however, Liele himself is buried in an unmarked grave in Jamaica.

Lamentations incorporates a myriad of voices to strengthen the narrative of the suffering of God's people. The vast array of voices reflected in Lamentations deepens our appreciation of the lament over fallen Jerusalem. The power of Lamentations is that the voices of those who have actually suffered are not missing. Unfortunately, George Liele's story is often absent from our understanding of mission history. Liele's story reveals an example of hidden and untold stories in American Christianity. Despite preceding both William Carey and Adoniram Judson by at least a decade, the story of George Liele remains largely unknown. Why does Liele remain unsung as the first American missionary? Ultimately, I believe that the inability to embrace the story of George Liele reveals the inability of the majority culture to embrace a nontraditional story outside the parameters of the majority-culture Christianity. It is human tendency to bias and privilege our own history and our own point of view. There are minimal consequences to not knowing another's history. In Lamentations 2, we discover the power of a multitude of voices from a wide range, offered collectively. It does not seek to present only the celebration culture of the wealthy and the powerful. Instead, it offers a myriad of voices, including those who suffer.

In the same way, the twenty-first-century Western church could broaden the voices that are heard in our Christian expression. Christian conferences in the United States could certainly benefit from a greater diversity of voices. The type and origin of the songs that are sung in our worship life could also draw from a myriad of voices. What we surround ourselves with, in our everyday and communal Christian life, should reflect a commitment to hear the multitude of voices. The normative expression of Christian faith should arise from a life lived with hearing from a range of voices, experiences and stories.

When a couple in the United States prepares for a crosscultural adoption, a training program is required before the event. One such exercise during this training involves a glass bowl with a vast array of marbles. The couple is asked a series of questions that help capture the voices and influences that shape their home life. In response to these questions, they are asked to add to their glass bowl a marble whose color best corresponds to the questions. For example, a white couple was asked: Who are the last three families you have had over for dinner? Three white marbles would go in the bowl. What color represents the faces that dominate the magazines in your home? More white marbles would go in the bowl. What type of music do you listen to? What TV shows do you watch? What movies do you watch? Who are the authors of the last ten books you have read? At the end of the process, a couple's bowl is filled to the brim with white marbles. The couple is then asked to drop the "color" of their baby into the same bowl—usually resulting in a single black marble in a bowl full of white marbles.

Lamentations presents a multitude of voices. The variety of voices reflecting a variety of experiences from a range of sources challenges us to broaden the voices that we hear in the formation of our spiritual lives and our Christian community.

HOPE ARISING FROM LAMENT

The final section of the second poem in the book of Lamentations offers a prayer to God that reveals an underlying hope. Even in this horrid situation, the exiles can hope in God's righteousness. God has revealed his faithfulness to the covenant by enacting judgment in response to covenant unfaithfulness. God has shown his character to be one of fidelity and justice. God is true to his nature and takes sin seriously. Justice is enacted against injustice and infidelity because God is true to his character and to the covenant. Because of his faithfulness to the curses associated with the covenant, there emerges a hope that God will be faithful to the promise of restoration. God's mercy is understood in light of God's justice. Not only has God shown his faithfulness, but also he has demonstrated his sovereignty. Trust in God's sovereignty leads to a hope in new life and transformation ordained by God. This new life is characterized by the shalom of God. Randy Woodley notes that

> the kind of peace shalom represents is active and engaged. . . . Shalom is communal, holistic and tangible. There is no private or partial shalom. The whole community must have shalom or no one has shalom. . . . Shalom is not for the many, while a few suffer; nor is it for the few while many suffer.[10]

The type of hope offered in Lamentations is a shalom hope that is not limited to human expectations.

O'Connor notes that "although laments appear disruptive of God's world, they are acts of fidelity."[11] God's actions in Lamentations 2 reveal his covenant faithfulness. While hope is not explicitly offered, there is an understanding that hope is available for those who trust in him. God is faithful to judge; God will be faithful to restore. As O'Connor summarizes,

> Laments are prayers of the discontented, the disturbed, and the distraught. . . . But remarkably, in the process of harsh complaint and resistance, they also express faith in God in the midst of chaos, doubt, and confusion. . . . The lament forms themselves alert readers that, no matter the complaint, the poems emerge from profound "disorientation" to life.[12]

The absence of explicit hope in the book of Lamentations does not diminish the existence of a very real hope underneath the surface of real suffering.

In *The Sacrifice of Africa*, Emmanuel Katongole presents stories of the church that exemplify a type of insanity that arises out of a deep-seated suffering but leads to profound reconciliation and healing. Each story reveals a type of revolutionary madness that arises out of a history of suffering. Yet this revolutionary madness finds expression in the narrative of the church and provides an "interruption of the social history shaped by tribalism, poverty, violence, and hatred."[13] The madness of suffering has found expression, not for further destruction but for reconciliation.

The church has the power to bring healing in a racially fragmented society. That power is not found in an emphasis on strength but in suffering and weakness. The difficult topic of racial reconciliation requires the intersection of celebration and suffering. The Lord's Table provides the opportunity for the church to operate at the intersection of celebration and suffering. In 1 Corinthians 11:26, we are reminded that we have the opportunity to "proclaim the Lord's death." In remembering Jesus' suffering on our behalf, we discover our mutual and common dependence on the body of Christ broken for us. It is not merely the symbolic act of the Lord's Table that unites us, but the commitment to that broken body and the actual embodiment of unity. The suffering narrative that informs the Lord's Table is essential for the unity found in the body of Christ. The necessary condition for the celebration of the Lord's Supper, therefore, is lament.

Lamentations recognizes that hope can arise in the midst of suffering because of God's faithfulness. Celebration can arise out of suffering, but lament is a necessary expression of that suffering. In a triumphalistic world, Lamentations makes no sense. The theology of celebration will always be more attractive than the theology of suffering. But if lament were offered to a suffering world, the hope that is woven into lament offers the possibility of genuine reconciliation.

Lamentations 3

I grew up in two streams of American Christianity that tend to eschew tradition and liturgy. In the Southern Baptist church of my childhood, I was taught that traditional liturgy was not to be trusted since it reflected the stodgy practices of a bygone era. As a member of a charismatic church in my youth and early adulthood, I was taught that tradition and liturgy stifle the creativity and freedom offered in the spontaneity of contemporary, charismatic worship and prayer. The church of my youth and my young adulthood offered the experience of freedom necessary for my spiritual journey. Spontaneous spirituality through contemporary worship and charismatic expressions of prayer helped to alleviate teenage angst and family tensions.

In my present context, liturgical worship dominates as the central form of worship. I am challenged by the notion that structure and tradition serve as key elements of corporate worship. I am further intrigued by how evangelicalism can hold seemingly disparate expressions of worship in dynamic tension and even fullness of expression. While the breadth of evangelicalism can encompass the range of worship expressions, worship preferences in the local church tend to reflect whether the congregation arises from the context of celebration versus suffering.

Churches that operate under the theology of celebration tend to engage in liturgy, tradition and structure in worship. The reenacting of a historical tradition may reflect the desire of a celebrating community to maintain the status quo and a systematized form of worship that affirms existing value systems. The opposite tendency exists for churches operating under the theology of suffering. For example, spontaneous worship in the Pentecostal tradition reflects its early roots, which arose out of a ministry toward the marginalized and disenfranchised. Freedom of expression and spontaneity in worship arises from a desire to oppose the status quo and the structures that sustain the existing systems of injustice.

The range of expressions in worship emerges from a range of life circumstances and experiences. Often, we trivialize worship differences or stereotype the sides that have become entrenched in the worship wars. Worship differences are simplistically defined as a personal preference for contemporary Christian music over traditional hymns. But there needs to be recognition of the underlying value system and ethos that shapes worship styles. Through that recognition, there could be a deeper understanding and appreciation of the other.

I find myself wanting to experience the fullness of both celebration and suffering. I find myself wanting to move between all of the streams of my childhood, youth and current context. I hope to find the power of the combination of spontaneity that reflects a spirituality that is sensitive to the Spirit and spiritual rootedness in a rich historical tradition. Lamentations 3 offers a form of worship that operates within the boundaries of faith but also reveals a deeply experienced and lived faith. It accounts for tradition *and* spontaneity.

A Structure for Lament

The Use of the Acrostic in Lamentations

Lamentations 3 serves as the height and climax of the book of Lamentations. It recapitulates key elements of the previous chapters but with a heightened intensity, and expresses the depth and breadth of emotion within proper structural boundaries. The genre, form and content of the third poem aid in the expression of deep emotions experienced by God's people.

Throughout the book of Lamentations, the author employs the poetic form of the acrostic. The first four chapters of Lamentations are written in the form of an alphabet acrostic with each verse beginning with a different letter of the Hebrew alphabet in alphabetical order. The fifth chapter is a "weak" acrostic that presents twenty-two verses reflecting the number of letters in the Hebrew alphabet but with the first letter of each verse not presented in alphabetical order.

Chapters 1 and 2 presents twenty-two verses of three lines each with each verse beginning with a letter in alphabetic order. For example, translated into the English, verse 1 of chapters 1 and 2 begins with the letter *A* with three lines, and verse 2 continues with the letter *B*.

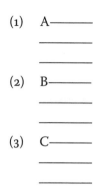

(1)   A———

     ———

     ———

(2)   B———

     ———

     ———

(3)   C———

     ———

     ———

Chapter 4 presents twenty-two verses of two lines each in alphabetical order.

(1)   A———

     ———

(2)   B———

     ———

(3)   C———

     ———

Chapter 5 presents twenty-two verses not in alphabetical order as a "weak" acrostic.

(1)   Z———
(2)   N———
(3)   I———

Chapter 3, however, presents an intensification of the alphabet acrostic producing sixty-six verses with each letter of the alphabet repeated three times.

(1)   A———
(2)   A———
(3)   A———
(4)   B———

(5)   B———

(6)   B———

(7)   C———

(8)   C———

(9)   C———

The middle chapter of Lamentations, therefore, displays the intensification of the acrostic form.

The last two chapters of Lamentations exhibit a declining intensity, hinting that chapter 3 presents an intentional climax for the book of Lamentations. Chapter 3, therefore, offers a recapitulation of the main themes already presented in the first two chapters of the book: YHWH's anger against Jerusalem (v. 1), YHWH's rejection (v. 2), YHWH's judgment (v. 3), the subsequent sense that YHWH is now Israel's enemy (vv. 10-13) and the consequent suffering of Jerusalem (vv. 15-16, 19-20). The intensified acrostic of Lamentations 3 draws attention to the key themes of rejection, loss and lament.

Theories abound regarding the intention of the use of the alphabet acrostic. The range of possible options include the use of the acrostic as a magic formula, or as a pedagogic or mnemonic device. While the didactic and mnemonic purpose may have been a factor in the use of the acrostic, the

> more evocative and symbolic purposes may better explain the use of alphabet in Lamentations. Acrostics impose order and organization on shapeless chaos and unmanageable pain, and they imply that the suffering depicted in the poems is total. Nothing can be added to it, for suffering extends from "A to T" (*aleph* to *taw*) [the first letter of the Hebrew alphabet to the last].[1]

The boundaries of the acrostic form provide a sense of completion. Lamentations 3, therefore, provides an intensified version of the acrostic in presenting the full spectrum of the Hebrew alphabet in triplicate. The chaos that is consistently portrayed in the book of Lamentations finds focus and shape through the acrostic. Lamentations does not hold back its depiction of suffering, and in order to provide a comprehensive account of suffering, Lamentations employs the help of the acrostic.

Suffering expressed in Lamentations runs deep. Experiencing deep suffering pushes the individual and community in multiple directions, sometimes without constraints. Lamentations' use of the acrostic offers the possibility of full disclosure, but in a safe place. Gottwald states that

> those who entertain this idea of completeness, therefore, instinctively feel that in naming the whole alphabet one comes as close as man may to a total development of any theme or the complete expression of any emotion or belief. If the subject is to be exhausted, the alphabet alone can suffice to suggest and symbolize the totality striven after.[2]

Deep suffering can result in a deep despair, unless the boundaries of suffering are laid out. "In Lamentations, the impression is rather of a boundless grief, an over-flowing emotion, whose expression benefits from the limits imposed by a confining acrostic form, as from the rather tightly fixed metrical pattern."[3]

Unfettered suffering devastates a fragile soul and a fragile community. "Aesthetically, it seems that the somewhat rigid bounds which the acrostic sets contribute a desirable limit to a subject matter that might otherwise run on and on."[4] By expressing the fullness of grief from A to Z, the author of Lamentations seeks "that the people might experience an emotional catharsis. He wanted to bring about a complete cleansing of the conscience through a total confession of sin."[5] The acrostic guarantees that in some form, the full account of their suffering will be expressed. The totality of suffering must be expressed. In order to fully express that suffering, Lamentations must offer the boundaries and parameters that offer a comprehensive account of suffering. The acrostic presents a form that allows suffering to take shape. "The function of the acrostic was to encourage completeness in the expression of grief, the confession of sin and the instilling of hope."[6] The full expression of grief is now evident in the context of worship through the acrostic formula. The boundaries offered by the acrostic provide the liturgical space to fully express lament.

As discussed in the introduction, many American churches steeped in the theology of celebration lack lament as an expression of worship. This absence of lament is attributable in part to the denial of suffering, the fear of what an unfettered suffering may mean to the community and the lack of the practice of lament causing one to forget its importance. The acrostic helps to address many of these gaps in our expression of lament. Lament is truth telling, and the acrostics provide safe boundaries and guidelines where truth can be expressed. Lament as expressed through the acrostic provides the surety to express the fullness of suffering but within the prescribed form. Expressed properly, the familiarity of the acrostic should free the lamenter to engage in the ongoing practice of lament. The acrostic formula offers the liturgical structure within which the fullness of suffering can be expressed as lament.

ORDER BEYOND OUR CHAOS

Even without liturgy, the fullness of suffering is easy to identify in urban ministry. Urban pastors are no strangers to suffering because urban ministry can often seem like a sea of chaos. We confront the youth group member who is about to be initiated into a gang. We address the special needs elementary school student about to be sent to a psych ward for children. We encounter the couple dealing with the demon of domestic violence. We support the young man who was recently released from prison and is looking for work. We comfort the senior citizen whose heat has been shut off. We aid the recently laid-off single mom about to lose her apartment. We accompany the family rushing to the hospital to be by the bedside of the teenage son who was the victim of gun violence. The list continues. It is unending. Suffering can seem unfettered in the daily life of the urban pastor; prayer and worship feel overwhelming and even unattainable as the list of challenges pile up.

In the midst of this chaos, some sort of spiritual order is sought. This kind of suffering is too overwhelming. We need to know that there is order beyond our present reality. The acrostic, therefore, points to an order beyond our chaos.

Dobbs-Allsopp claims: "the acrostic projects 'its formal order as a token, a security—something given in hand—to guarantee the cosmic order' beyond the turbulence of Jerusalem's historical reality."[7] The acrostic reminds the lamenter that God orders the universe. In the midst of chaos and beyond the immediacy of suffering, God demonstrates control. Even as the fullness of suffering is unleashed and the complete story is revealed, God remains faithful and offers his shalom to a broken world.

In Lamentations 3:1-20, we encounter once more the cries of the suffering. There is affliction (v. 1), an overwhelming presence of darkness (vv. 2, 6), physical pain (vv. 4, 11, 16), imprisonment (vv. 7, 9) and external threats (vv. 5, 10) with a corresponding loss of hope (vv. 18, 20). However, Lamentations 3 begins to offer the glimmer of hope starting with verse 21. This hope is found only through the faithfulness of YHWH (vv. 21-26) and moves toward a plea for the community to cry out to God (vv. 28-42). In these verses, we see how hope is restored. It is not by human effort (vv. 44-45) but by the grace of God. In the midst of the acrostic which allows for the full venting of a suffering people, God's covenant loyalty emerges. In the midst of urban ministry where the full expression of human suffering can occur,

God's covenant loyalty does not wane.

The possibility of ministry in the context of urban ministry is the possibility of the Christian community offering shalom within the full expression of suffering and grief. Lament presents the possibility of an order ordained by God in the midst of a broken reality. The excessive suffering of the first section of Lamentations 3 has found expression in the acrostic, and the community now seeks the security and hope that comes from God alone (vv. 21-29). The use of the acrostic together with the progression of Lamentations 3 reminds us that unfettered suffering gestures toward the shalom that God brings to his people. While the chapter begins with the experience of suffering, the covenant loyalty of God sits at the heart of the acrostic. The acrostic allows for both the full venting of lament but also gestures toward the possibility of shalom: that God will bring all things to his conclusion. The presence of the urban church can serve as an expression of security that God is in charge of the cosmic order beyond the turbulence of the urban reality. As an expression of God's will, the church in the city can embody God's shalom. It becomes the order of the acrostic in the sea of the chaos of suffering.

In my experience as an urban pastor, I have witnessed how the church finds itself in the midst of unfettered suffering. Often, this type of suffering (maybe best typified by violence against children and youth) leaves a community in disarray and in deep pain without any recourse. For a number of years I had the great honor of serving with a ministry that sought to curb youth violence in the city of Boston. The Boston TenPoint Coalition emerged in response to a violent action that occurred inside a church building. The street shooting of a gang member necessitated a funeral at a local Boston church. Unfortunately, violence extended into the church when a fight broke out between the rival gangs during the funeral, resulting in the stabbing death of another young man within the walls of the church. A group of African American pastors responded by recognizing that the church had not gone into the streets, so the streets had come into the church. The suffering in the city was unfettered. The church had failed to be the shalom in the city. Youth labeled as "at-risk" had not been welcomed in the church, nor were there any concerted efforts to conduct street outreach for youth.

The subsequent response of the African American churches in Boston was to begin a series of interventions to address youth violence. The initiatives led to the formation of the Boston TenPoint Coalition. Led by key African American church leaders, TenPoint employed multiple strategies to curb youth-related violence. School visits, home visits, nightly patrols, prayer vigils and cooperation with the police were all part of the strategy.

One specific effort focused on training ministers to deal with a traumatic loss in the community. The training equips pastors to be present at gang-related funerals. Pastors and church leaders serve as spiritual counselors and as a spiritual presence during a time of deep grief and trauma. Pastors also serve as a nonanxious presence during a time of great anxiety and tension. The initial incident that sparked the formation of the TenPoint Coalition would not be repeated. Christian leaders served as the peacemakers during moments of deep suffering and potential violence. The church had become a safe place so that suffering could be expressed and shalom could be pursued.

Another initiative took seriously the effort to bring the church to the streets. I was honored to participate in the home-visit initiative, which paired two police officers with two members of the clergy. The clergy sat in the back of the police car behind the metal grate as we drove around the neighborhood. The team of four would then visit the home of a youth offender who had been tagged by the system for getting into a fight at school, bringing a weapon to school or sporting gang colors and insignia. When the police knocked on the door, the door remained locked. When the pastor knocked on the door, someone would usually open the door for the group. Through the visitation, the police and the clergy enacted the classic bad cop/good pastor routine; the young offender was confronted with his actions but was also offered the opportunity to connect with local law enforcement *and* local clergy. Through this effort, boundaries of hostility and mistrust were broken between youth, the church and the local police. The young offender was allowed to give voice to the clergy about his story of suffering. Space was created for lament to be expressed, for the answer to be sought outside of the suffering reality and in turn, shalom became a possibility.

TenPoint entered into partnerships with local law enforcement to quell the anxiety and mistrust of the community toward the police. TenPoint pastors were long-standing members of the Boston Christian community. They possessed integrity derived from indigenous leadership stemming from deep roots in the community. And these pastors gave the police credibility in their work with the community. The community was allowed to express the full extent of their trauma, and police brutality was no longer tolerated because the community had a voice through the activist pastors. The stories of suffering were no longer hidden as the pastors advocated for the sufferers to fully express themselves. The pastors became the shalom presence in the community, bringing peace and comfort in the midst of great turmoil and suffering.

The work of TenPoint Coalition has been applauded as a positive example of addressing youth gang violence. During the most active years of the Boston TenPoint Coalition in the 1990s, the Boston homicide rate dropped a full 80 percent. Youth-related gun violence took a particularly sharp downward turn.[8] Many hailed the cooperative work of the police, the community and the church as the "Boston Miracle." Rather than hiding inside the confines of the four walls of a building, the church became the expression of God's shalom on the streets. The church became the place where genuine grief and pain and suffering could be safely and fully expressed. The church also became the nonanxious and peaceful presence in the midst of suffering, the living embodiment of Christ. The church became the living acrostic in the sea of chaos.

In Lamentations 3, the use of the acrostic affirms the necessity of the presence of shalom and a faithful structure that creates room for that presence. Western churches often present modes of worship that elevate celebration over suffering. The corrective of lament must be intentionally built into the structures of liturgy and worship life. What songs can be sung that would reflect the reality of suffering in the world? What prayers of lament can be offered that respond to the pain found in our communities? How can small groups and Bible studies become embodied acrostics providing room for engagement with the narrative of suffering? But furthermore, how could the practice of our worship, prayer and study lead to the embodiment of the acrostic in our world? In similar fashion to the work of the TenPoint Coalition, could churches take the presence of shalom into the community and offer a hope that arises from the full expression of God's shalom?

ALL OF IT IS PERSONAL

Lamentations 3

Lamentations 3 begins with an introduction of a prophet speaking in the first-person singular. We have asserted that the prophet-narrator in Lamentations is either the voice of Jeremiah himself or someone approximating his voice and perspective, since this voice fulfills the role of a prophet. One of the key roles of the prophet is to serve as a covenant mediator between God and his people. Jeremiah enforces the covenant by presenting God's perspective (e.g., Lam 2:1-8) while at the same time reflecting the voice of the people (Lam 3:1-20).

Lamentations 3 reveals the heart of a prophet who offers a personal lament on behalf of the community. In contrast to the earlier chapters, Lamentations 3 shifts from a third-person to a first-person singular account of the fall of Jerusalem. By shifting this voice, Lamentations 3 transitions from a funeral dirge to a personal lament offered on behalf of the entire community.

Jeremiah's personal lament contrasts with laments that focus on individual suffering. In Lamentations 3, Jeremiah offers a personal reflection revealing a connection to the community's experience.

The prophet places his story in the context of the community's story of suffering. This level of corporate empathy contrasts to an individualism that focuses on one's individual experience, offering instead a lament on behalf of the entire community.

Personal lament not only reveals the personal struggle of the individual, but reflects communal emotions and experiences. The interplay of the individual and the corporate voice is found in the genre of praise as well as lament. Westermann notes that even "in the voice of an individual the community proclaims before the world what God has done. . . . The proper witness to the deeds of God occurs in the existence of the community in the world."[1] In the expression of praise in the Psalms, the individual is never an isolated individual, but instead reveals praise emerging out of the context of the entire community.

In the same way that personal praise is not an isolated experience, personal laments do not operate solely in the realm of individual suffering. The personal laments in Lamentations point to the communal grieving experienced by the entire community but expressed by the individual. A modern example of this was when a congregant in my church wrote a deeply personal lament song revealing her personal sorrow and grief after the tragic events of 9/11. The song presented a personal testimony performed by an individual. There was great value and beauty in the personal expression of sorrow, but this personal expression reflected the sorrow of the entire community, and in turn the community identified with the very personal song of the individual. Like Jeremiah, that individual sang a personal song on behalf of the whole community.

In Lamentations 3:1, the prophet-narrator is "the man who has seen affliction by the rod of the LORD's wrath." The "rod of the LORD's wrath" implies the full strength of God's anger in the severity and overwhelming nature of his response. O'Connor notes that "has seen" in verse 1 can also mean "to experience," which shows how the prophet-narrator "embodies the community's massive suffering."[2] In verse 2, there is the painful experience of exile where "He has driven me away and made me walk in darkness rather than light." Even though Jeremiah has been left in Jerusalem to witness her downfall, he envisions himself suffering as those who have been driven away into exile. In verse 3, YHWH "has turned his hand against me / again and again, all day long." Instead of experiencing the gentle hand of God, the prophet now experiences the punishing hand of God. In verse 4, the entirety of his body, "my skin and my flesh . . . my bones," is impacted. The totality of the impact by the judgment of God is expanded upon in verse 5 where he is besieged and surrounded and in verse 7 where he is walled in and weighed down.

The experience described by Jeremiah in these first seven verses reflects similar wording to the description of the experience by Jerusalem during the siege. Like the city, the prophet's wounds are both external and internal (v. 4). He has been besieged and encompassed (v. 5). He has been walled in so that he cannot go out (v. 7). His way has been blocked with a heavy stone (v. 9). The prophet's personal experience echoes the horror of the besieged city. The prophet's fate is the same as the city herself. His pain is her pain.

The prophet feels the bodily assault of being dragged and mangled (v. 11). His heart (v. 13) and his teeth (v. 16) are assaulted. Lamentations 3:1-20 is filled with images of an attack on the prophet narrator's person and body. This personal physical assault leads to isolation as his cries and prayers are not heard (v. 8). He is mocked (v. 14) and filled with bitterness and gall (v. 19), culminating in a downcast soul (v. 20). Lamentations 3:1-20 is a comprehensive account of the suffering experienced by God's people, including an account that reflects the experience of a personified Jerusalem.

Suffering and pain are not isolated to the individual experience, so Lamentations employs both a personal and corporate voice, oftentimes woven together. Personal reflection on communal suffering reflects an important movement in the book of Lamentations.

Suffering, therefore, is not merely something to be observed from a distance as a third-person observer or as a depersonalized communal lament, but as a first-person experience expressed as a personal lament.

While Jeremiah empathizes with the suffering of his community, his personal lament offered in Lamentations 3 does not necessarily arise out of a personal culpability in the sin that led to the fall of Jerusalem. In fact, Jeremiah's voice would have been the one voice that remained faithful to God's words. Despite Jeremiah's relative innocence to the rest of the community, he embraces his role as a prophet who speaks for his people, offering a lament on behalf of the people and speaking the experience of the Jerusalem community. Up until Lamentations 3, the prophet-narrator has been an almost dispassionate observer, reporting on the horrors experienced by the citizens of Jerusalem. A shift seems to occur when he expresses a more personal connection with the suffering citizens of Jerusalem.

This connection to the guilt of the citizens of Jerusalem contrasts to Jeremiah's actual story. The one individual in the exile story that can claim innocence is the prophet Jeremiah. Jeremiah faithfully spoke YHWH's words and remained faithful both to YHWH and to the covenant. Yet, Jeremiah claims a personal connection to the sins of his community. He experiences the same suffering as his community (vv. 1-20), and he also participates in a corporate call for repentance in Lamentations 3:40-42 in stating: "Let us examine our ways and test them, / and let us return to the LORD. / Let us lift up our hearts and our hands to God in heaven and say: / 'We have sinned and rebelled / and you have not forgiven.'" We find this pattern not only in Lamentations but also in Jeremiah 14:20 as Jeremiah states: "We acknowledge our wickedness, LORD, / and the guilt of our ancestors; / we have indeed sinned against you." Jeremiah could legitimately claim innocence, but instead chose to embrace the corporate sin of his community and to express that culpability through the individual lament of Lamentations 3. What affected Jerusalem on a corporate level has affected Jeremiah on an individual level. He empathizes to the point of offering a confession for sins committed by the community. And as he offers up a confession, he speaks corporately on behalf of the sufferers.

American society tends toward a hyperindividualistic narrative. Our expressions of worship and our religious practices focus on individual experience and choice. Personal freedom and the primacy of the individual rule our understanding of how society functions. But a hyperindividualistic ethos results in a disengagement with the reality of corporate sin. Social injustice is dismissed to focus solely on individual expressions of sin. This process relegates the role of the church exclusively to a hyperindividualistic expression. Sin has been reduced to an individual level.

Corporate sin, however, must be acknowledged. In the same way that Jeremiah acknowledges corporate responsibility and offers a prayer of confession for "our" sin, we are challenged to understand the corporate aspects of human sinfulness. Jeremiah sets an example of the prophetic call to empathize with the people. How are twenty-first-century Christians embracing that prophetic role? How are we moving beyond the hyperindividualism of the culture to follow the biblical example of Lamentations? Our society struggles not only with the actions of individuals but the larger social impact of their actions. In the same way personal prejudice can lead to structural racism, personal actions have corporate implications. But this corporate understanding of injustice will require an understanding of the impact of corporate injustice on the realm of the individual. When an individual receives privileges and benefits from an unjust system, or contributes (even if it is unwittingly) to perpetuate an unjust system, then there is individual responsibility for corporate injustice. Jeremiah offers an example of a prophet whose suffering parallels Jerusalem's suffering but whose corporate confession rises up on behalf of his people.

An additional role of the prophet is to stand as an advocate for others. The advocate role is an important role in the ministry of justice. Many American Christians hold a position of privilege in American society. Part of that privilege is the ability to claim a degree of innocence as Jeremiah would have been able. As the privileged, there is an important voice that can be raised on behalf of the marginalized and the suffering. American Christians can advocate for the rights of the unborn, the poor and the oppressed of our society. Part of our call to be a prophetic presence is to advocate for change that benefits the very least of our brothers and sisters. Jeremiah takes on the suffering experiences of others and offers a confession for sins that he himself may not have committed. Jeremiah sets an example for those of us who may claim innocence or hold positions of privilege. Jeremiah lives into the role of the prophet by empathizing with and advocating for the sufferers in Jerusalem.

There are, however, limits to the role of the advocate since he or she is not in a position of superiority over the suffering. We observe Jeremiah putting himself into the depths of suffering. He does not claim a superiority but instead seeks to accurately reflect the stories of those in his community. The advocate must never replace the voice of the suffering, especially when the suffering people seek to speak for themselves. Part of the role of the advocate in American society is to help the voiceless gain their own voice. The prophet's voice is not to be asserted over and above that of the suffering community. Instead, like Jeremiah in Lamentations 3, the modern-day prophet can empathize and advocate.

Jeremiah's perspective does not limit the suffering of Jerusalem to abstract terms; what Jerusalem has experienced Jeremiah experiences on a personal level. Even the most abstract and corporate sin is personal. A personal experience runs deeper. Abstract terms like *poverty, justice* or *urban ministry* can ring shallow as a rallying cry. Concrete expressions such as "Fred is hungry," "Malik is homeless"

or "Maria has been kicked out of her home" have a greater impact.
A greater sense of responsibility is demanded when Jeremiah con-
cretizes his suffering since it is no longer a distant, objective reality
but a personal experience. Jeremiah does not merely see the fallen
city in abstract terms, he embodies the suffering.

The hyperindividualism of Western culture also shapes how an
individual understands sin through a guilt orientation. Sin is reduced to a purely personal and individual expression. Release from
the guilt of that individual sin comes through a personal confession
and the subsequent sense of relief from a clear conscience. Many
non-Western cultures operate out of a corporate shame orientation.
Shame does not limit sin to an individual action but focuses on
one's identity. Shame arises out of a corporate context and one's
relationship to that corporate context. Therefore, shame is not absolved by simply confessing sin; it requires a transformation before
the community and accountability within that context.

Recently, I attended a conference on Native American theology.
One of the white participants at the conference suggested that we do
away with words like *Christian* and *evangelical* because they have
too strong of a negative connotation. He claimed that we needed to
reject the words and the baggage that comes with those words. A
Native American theologian responded that doing away with those
words would prove to be convenient for the majority culture. Not
only would the words be wiped away, but the responsibility for the
negative history of those communities could also be wiped away. Sin
would not be accounted for.

Some want to do away with cultural differences and wipe away
the long historical problem of race. With the election of Obama,
America has supposedly moved toward a postracial world. But a
robust dialogue on race requires a sense of personal culpability.
There needs to be a personal connection to the corporate sin that
has entered our culture. Our claims must first shift from the de-

fensive posture of "I am not a racist" to "I am responsible and culpable in the corporate sin of racism." We must move from "let's just get over it" to "how do I personally continue to perpetuate systems of privilege?" Justice must move from the third person to the first person, from the abstract to the personal.

A Glimmer of Hope

Lamentations 3:21-60

After vivid descriptions of misery and suffering for two chapters and the first part of Lamentations 3, a positive expression of hope is finally offered. Verse 21 offers the prophet's hope: "Yet this I call to mind / and therefore I have hope," which could be paraphrased as: "I remember something that changed how I think, and now I have hope." Verse 21 is the third of three lines that begin with the Hebrew letter *zayin*. While structurally tied to verses 19 and 20, verse 21 offers a seemingly abrupt change in the prophet's perspective. By invoking the phrase "This I call to mind," the prophet engages in a different train of thought.

After sixty-four verses of expressing deep suffering, hope is finally offered. This hope does not rely on human achievement or triumphalism, but instead on God's grace. The shift in verse 21 arises from a calling to mind of the faithfulness of God to his covenant. These verses do not emphasize the human ability to turn around their own circumstances but instead focus on the character of God to bring about change. Hope is dependent on who God *is* rather than what we can do for ourselves.

In verse 22, Lamentations reminds us that God is faithful. The Hebrew word *hesed* is usually translated simply as "mercy" or "compassion." In many cases, *hesed* should be understood as God's loyalty to his covenant. God does what he says he will do. In contrast to people, God does not act capriciously. In ministry, we are often hurt by people. Urban ministry is susceptible to those individuals who come and go from our outreach programs. They have great moments of spiritual renewal, only to return to sinful habits the next day. This capriciousness is not only symptomatic of urban churches but *all* churches, because human beings are fickle beings.

God's character is immutable. *Hesed* captures this essence. The justice that emerges from this covenant faithfulness is also immutable, which contrasts sharply with human fickleness. I am reminded of this reality as a parent. Based upon my actions as a parent, I would make a terrible judge since I can be very arbitrary. If my children don't walk the dog, they may be grounded for a month. Burning down the house might mean . . . no Xbox for a week. Maybe not to that extreme, but I am susceptible to a high level of inconsistency because I am human. My only consolation is that God does not operate under this same type of capriciousness in his judgment. Instead, he operates from loyalty to the covenant.

God's anger, therefore, is a temporary condition. His steadfast love and mercy persevere as primary characteristics. For God, covenant loyalty and fidelity are not based upon a feeling. Loyalty is "not a passing phase in God, but an enduring part of his nature, always being renewed toward mankind."[1] *Hesed* arises from a sense of obligation and fidelity. God is obligated toward us. While Western concepts of obligation may involve a sense of duty that minimizes feelings of love and affection, non-Western cultures move beyond a simplistic understanding of obligation. In fact, God's love is best revealed as a reflection of his fidelity. One of the most important and consistent expression of God's love is his *hesed*.

How God feels and acts toward us does not arise from our ability to behave in a certain way, but upon *his* fidelity to his own word and his unwavering loyalty. This realization of God's fidelity is reflected in the statement: "I thought." The lamenter had mistakenly thought one way about God, but is reminded that God is something else. The description of YHWH up to this point could be construed as negative, but that perception has now turned with this recollection and remembering of God's true character, faithfulness and goodness.

Delbert Hillers notes, "Not God's love, but his anger is a passing phase, and thus even of suffering the first word of faith can be 'Good'; the poet puts this 'good' (Heb *tōb*) at the beginning of the next three lines (vv. 25-27)."[2] Suffering, evil and pain are not YHWH's final intention. YHWH has the last word because his love is never finished. The narrator finds hope not in his own accomplishments or abilities to transcend suffering, but because of the faithful character of YHWH.

YHWH's covenant loyalty serves as the foundation for the additional attributes of God that furthers our hope in this section of Lamentations. God's loyalty to the covenant amplifies the power of the statements that "God's compassions [mercy] never fail" and "great is your faithfulness." In verse 22, God's compassion and mercy are highlighted through the use of the Hebrew word *rakham*. The *Theological Wordbook of the Old Testament* notes that the root word means to love deeply, to have mercy and be compassionate. "This root refers to deep love rooted in some 'natural' bond. In the Piel it is used for the deep inward feeling we know variously as compassion, pity, mercy."[3] In verse 23, the Hebrew word *'emunah* emphasizes God's faithfulness. "The term applies to God himself to express his total dependability."[4] Holladay's lexicon defines the semantic field for this term as the following: "prove oneself steady, reliable.... To have stability, remain, continue."[5] All three words—covenant loyalty, compassion, faithfulness—draw attention to God's character. God's character is revealed in how he relates to humanity, and his constancy is reflected in these three words. It is the revelation of YHWH's character that provides hope for his people.

Verses 28 to 30 again draw attention to God as the main actor in the process of the restoration of hope. While God's people are called to action, that action focuses on yielding to God's authority. The phrase "let him . . ." is repeated to call the people to submit to God. In the language of individual lament, the one who laments is commanded to "wait quietly / for the salvation of the Lord . . . bury his face in the dust . . . offer his cheek to one who would strike him, / and let him be filled with disgrace" (vv. 26, 29-30). Each command acknowledges God's just judgment and the need to submit to God's divine will and authority. In Lamentations, the people's hope is tied to submission to God, not to an assertion of their own abilities.

Confession and Redemption

In our engagement on issues of justice, do we rely too much on our own abilities rather than the character of God? This moment of acknowledging dependence on God in Lamentations 3 signals a moment of transition. As Dobbs-Allsopp notes, "Beginning here and carrying forward through the immediately following section there is a noticeable change in mood and feel."[6] Restoration and hope arise from a dependence on God's covenant loyalty that stems from his character.

The confirmation of God's character leads to the possibility of appealing to him. Equipped with a deep belief and faith in YHWH, the voice of Jeremiah moves toward a corporate confession of sin. In verse 40, there is a corporate self-examination: "Let us examine our ways and test them," followed by corporate repentance: "let us return to the Lord." Verses 41 and 42 follow with a corporate confession: "Let us lift up our hearts and our hands / to God in heaven, and say: / 'We have sinned and rebelled.'" Spiritual renewal emerges as God's people engage in a corporate confession of sin, and sincere repentance moves the community toward a changed and renewed life.

Historically, spiritual renewal movements are sparked by confession and repentance. Richard Lovelace points out that the preconditions for renewal involve the awareness of the holiness of God's justice and the awareness of the depth of sin in our own lives and in our community.[7] Confession propels the community to imagine a world beyond their current state of sinful existence. Lament that recognizes the reality of brokenness allows the community to express confession in its proper context. Confession acknowledges the need for God and opens the door for God's intervention. Confession in lament relies on God's work for redemption.

This section of Lamentations 3 continues the theological turning point of the book. "If God is indeed so good and so merciful, and if the people have sinned, the natural next step is that the people must repent and then they will surely be forgiven."[8] This section of Lamentations not only seeks individual redemption, but also calls for a corporate confession and redemption. The common thread in these verses is that they are all corporate, collective confessions. "This section is the theological and poetic turning point. These verses form a transition to a new type of discourse, in which the speaker is 'we' instead of 'I' and in which God is addressed directly as 'you' instead of being spoken about as 'he.'"[9] Repentance and confession are not simply offered for individual sins but also for the sins of the community. To move from the place of lament to the possibility of restoration, confession needs to be a part of the equation. Confession cannot be skipped in lament in order to get to the quick and easy solutions.

Lamentations 3 reminds us that confession should be offered not only on an individual level but also on a corporate level. The reality of corporate sin requires the power of corporate confession. As the nation of Israel sinned collectively before God, they must now offer a collective confession. If individuals have contributed to a system of injustice, confession of a sinful social system must be offered to address sin in its proper context. Recognition of corporate sin should lead to corporate confession.

In *Forgive Us*, my coauthors and I present the necessity of corporate confession for effective Christian witness.

> At this moment in history, the American church is often ridiculed or portrayed as unforgiving and ungracious. Could the church offer a counter-narrative, not of defensiveness or derision, but of an authentic confession and genuine reconciliation? . . . It is antithetical to the gospel when we do not confess all forms of sin—both individual and corporate. The reason evangelicals can claim to be followers of Jesus is because there has been an acknowledgement of sin and the seeking of God's grace through Jesus Christ that leads to the forgiveness of sin.[10]

Authentic witness that arises from lament requires a level of confession that has often been neglected. Confession must operate on all levels to bring healing and hope for forgiveness.

As the prophet-narrator offers a corporate confession, there is hope that God hears these cries. However, the immediate *feeling* of the confessor is that God has *not* heard these cries. The lamenter is distraught that "you have not forgiven. / You have covered yourself with anger. . . . You have covered yourself with a cloud / so that no prayer can get through" (vv. 42-44). Despite this confession, hope seems lost once more. One may note that this despair may have a reason; even as the lamenter directs a plea toward God, the enemy still surrounds (vv. 46, 52-53). Attention shifts from confession offered as a direct address to God to a focus on the circumstances of suffering and the pursuing enemies. The negative view of the world compels further pessimism about the situation. However, another shift occurs in the text as the lamenter turns once again to directly appeal to YHWH. "I called on your name. . . . You heard my plea. . . . You came near. . . . You, Lord, took up my case; / you redeemed my life. / You have seen. . . . You have seen" (vv. 55-60). Lamentations 3 offers the essential aspects of the liturgy of confession. True confession offered despite difficult circumstances is addressed to the only hope of our salvation: the God who sees, who acts and who brings redemption.

True Worship Arising from Suffering

Tisha B'Av is the day in the Jewish calendar that commemorates the destruction of both the first temple in 586 b.c. and the second temple in a.d. 70. In addition to the use of Lamentations to reflect on these historic events, Tisha B'Av commemorates the Roman massacre at Betar and the Bar Kochba fortress. "The Ninth Day of Av, is the day on which the Jewish people recall the catastrophes which it has suffered and which have influenced its life and character."[11] The ancient liturgy of Lamentations is read as part of the annual mourning and provides the framework by which suffering can be engaged. In the same way that the acrostic form allowed the mourners to express the fullness of their pain, sorrow and grief without completely losing their sanity, the liturgy of Tisha B'Av allows God's people to express pain without succumbing to total despair. Jewish scholars Morris and Hillel Silverman note that

> the Sages sought to make Tisha B'av a day on which the calamitous events of Jewish history would be remembered. Tisha B'av, marked by fasting and a special liturgy, was to be a time when Jews were to contemplate the disasters of their history, to mourn over them, and to resolve to help bring the redemption so that the sufferings would cease.[12]

The responsive reading for the Tisha B'Av liturgy ultimately concludes with reflections on the Holocaust. "Alas [an exclamation of despair], no generation has known a catastrophe so vast and tragic!

. . . Countless cities of slaughter from which six million of our
people were driven into a ghastly crematoria where they perished.
. . . We have witnessed the darkest chapter of Jewish history." The
immense suffering of the Holocaust meant the destruction of not
just one city but multiple cities of Jews. The level of grief and pain
resulting from this event requires the liturgical pattern of lament
to be able to express it.

Within Judaism, there was a movement to do away with this
particular ceremony. "Since the establishment of the reborn State
of Israel in 1948 there have been some who have felt that Tisha B'av
should no longer be observed."[13] Questions arose whether the
social and economic uplift experienced by many Jews diminished
the necessity to commemorate and lament a painful historical
event. Should the practice of lament be done away with now that
the events of the past no longer seem relevant to the present?

The American evangelical tendency also falls along these lines.
We do not need to engage in a suffering narrative in our worship
because we have achieved so much as an American church. We
have built megachurches, sent missionaries all over the world and
written countless Christian bestsellers. Why do we need to lament
in light of this triumphant narrative for the American church?
Rabbi Morris Silverman and Rabbi Hillel Silverman challenge us to
continue to intersect the suffering narrative with the celebratory
narrative. "It behooves us, even in triumph, to remember the days
of our degradation. It is important even for a reborn Israel to remember the sufferings of the past. It would be a severe diminishing
of our concern and love for those who went before us to remove
this day when their sufferings are recalled."[14]

One of the gifts of Pentecostal forms of worship is the depth of
emotions that arise from the context of suffering. Historically, Pentecostalism has drawn from urban settings, from the poor and disenfranchised of the community. Worship that encompasses the

breadth of emotion and corresponds to the breadth of suffering is an important expression of complete worship.

Lament allows for the *fullness* of emotions to be expressed. Worship should not operate with divergent goals, moving the community toward either celebration or suffering. They are not part of a zero-sum equation. Suffering and celebration must continue to intersect in our communities. Diverse worship expressions arising out of a range of experiences provide the opportunity to intersect the wide range of expressions that reflect the fullness of God's shalom.

Lamentations 4

During one of the more intense periods in the writing of this book, I entered into a week of what I can only describe as a time of depression. I don't think of myself as a depressive personality, so the entire week caught me a bit off-guard. I experienced a deep sense of sorrow that I could not shake. For even a brief moment, I experienced a glimpse of the depth of lament, an angst, a spiritual dis-ease that impacted every facet of my life. It was not an emotion that could be easily manipulated or explained away. There was no quick getting over it or "manning up" and moving on. Not even video games with my son could minimize this angst. There was only this profound sense that something was not quite right.

Part of the struggle during that week was that I was researching the section for this book on Nazi Germany and the German church's complicity in the rise of the Nazi party. I saw images of Christian pastors doing the "Heil Hitler" salute alongside SS officers. I saw an image of a German Christian academic who had grown a mustache to look exactly like Adolf Hitler's. I read about the horrific apathy and even participation of the German church that gave justification to genocide. The historical failure of the German church compelled me to reflect on the ongoing failures of the American church in the twentieth and twenty-first centuries. The church is Christ's bride. The church offers hope for a broken world. The church should embody the fullness of God's presence and should express God's shalom. But the church often does not live up to this promise. We've exchanged the glory of God for the lies of this earth. It was an easy journey to become depressed about the current state of the church. Lament emerged as an uncomfortable but necessary response to the absence of shalom in the church.

During another phase in the writing of this book, I experienced back-to-back personal losses, the second of which was my close friend and mentor, Richard Twiss, a Native American theologian who had profoundly shaped my Christian life. His too-early death brought about a deep need for self-examination leading to a series of questions and doubts about the trajectory of the American evangelical church. How can the church in America continue along a path that does not embrace the possibility of shalom? How can the message of my friend and mentor be ignored while the vacuous musings of the latest hotshot pastor garner undeserved attention? My depression arose out of a deep-seated frustration. Even as I write these sentences, I fight the urge to pound my desk and shout: "Wake up evangelicals! Stop wasting your time, energy and money on hipster Christianity in whatever nomenclature it operates under these days. Listen and learn from your Native American, African American, Latino/a brothers and sisters." There is so much God has in store for American Christians, but the frustration rises as we fall so far short of this possibility. Things are not the way they should be.

Both the struggle and liberation of the book of Lamentations is in knowing that there can be complete honesty before God. God's grace provides us the freedom to recognize that we fall short of the glory of God and that we will continue to do so. This side of heaven, we are confronted with the need to lament over a church that fails to live up to God's standards. But that failure ultimately results in a freedom to believe in the hope of God's restoration. Acknowledging the culpability of the American evangelical church in the history of racial injustice or recognizing our failure to confront systemic injustice is not a fruitless exercise. This process is not dwelling on the problem or failing to "get over it." It is the very real recognition that sin has wreaked havoc with our existing systems and structures and that we fail to measure up to God's value system. We must confess our desire to set up human standards of success over God's standards. We do not define shalom, God does.

Lamentations 4 deepens our understanding of God's value system. When God acts against Jerusalem, his actions could be interpreted as disrespectful. Such "disrespect" demonstrates God's elevated position over and above humanity. What should God respect? Who should God respect? Lamentations 4 reminds us that God does not respect what we respect. Our concerns are not God's concerns. Our values are not his values. American Christianity's captivity to Western cultural values and the ongoing commitment to those values have shaped how we define success. And that definition has been shaped by an American cultural value system more than the values of YHWH. But God has a very different definition of success.

Lamentations is a reminder of our place in creation. We are not elevated above God or even above God's creation. We do not stand in the place of Christ, able to incarnate ourselves into another community as if we could operate as the Messiah. Our only hope for meaning and worth is in the fullness of Christ as God's created beings. Lament recognizes our frailty as created beings and the need to acknowledge this shortcoming before God. Lament demands that we are willing to dwell in the space of our humanity without quickly resorting to our triumphalistic narrative to justify our worth.

PERSISTING IN LAMENT

A Recapitulation of Lamentations

After three chapters of lament, most of the major themes have been covered. Lamentations 4 offers a recapitulation of the key themes, but in a minor key as it moves toward a denouement after the climactic intensity of the previous chapter. The city-lament, funeral-dirge and communal-lament genres reappear to echo the same approach on key themes from previous chapters.

Thus far in Lamentations, we have heard the full expression of suffering experienced by God's people. No punches are pulled in the tragically vivid description of Israel's destruction. The death of the city is very real, and a funeral dirge is necessary to respond to the tragedy. To express the full range of suffering experienced in the fall of the city requires the full range of voices to express lament. The myriad of voices reveal the breadth of this tragedy and allow the entire community to speak a communal lament. Through the full expression of suffering by the city, we are given glimmers of hope—not hope in human abilities to fix the city, but in God's faithfulness to restore the city. Lamentations 4 recapitulates these major themes.

The reality of a fallen city still preoccupies the focus of the book as the city lament continues. Dobbs-Allsopp asserts that the city lament serves as the larger genre overarching the other genres.[1] The city-lament genre incorporates various elements of dirge, communal lament and individual lament. As O'Connor states:

> When the poet or poets of Lamentations sought to give expressions to the unspeakable pain their community endured, they drew on the repertoire of form, imagery, and metaphor available in the ancient world. From this familiar and traditional raw material, they created a complex artistic expression in the interplay of acrostic, lament, and dirge.[2]

The city lament incorporates multiple layers of the lament genre to reflect on the destruction of the city. Jerusalem remains central to the story of Lamentations; the city provides a key character in the poems as well as providing the scenery for the expression of lament.

The prophet-narrator consistently references urban life in setting the scene for Lamentations 4 where much of the action occurs on the "street." The text speaks of "every street" (v. 1), "in the streets" (vv. 5, 8), "through the streets" (v. 14) and "in our streets" (v. 18). The text also uses the physical structures of Jerusalem/Zion as a backdrop with references to "her foundations" (v. 11), the "gates of Jerusalem" (v. 12) and "our towers" (v. 17). There is also a reference to cities that are outside of Israel's covenant with YHWH, citing "Sodom" (v. 6) and "Daughter Edom" (v. 21). The city-lament genre is explicitly retained into Lamentations 4, a genre that does not back down from displaying the reality of a suffering city.

Also retained is the use of the acrostic formula. As stated previously, the acrostic pattern dominates the book of Lamentations. Lamentations 1–3 employ strong acrostics with an intensified acrostic in Lamentations 3 where each letter of the Hebrew alphabet starts three consecutive lines. Lamentations 4 uses a less intense acrostic with each letter of the Hebrew alphabet used every two lines, and Lamentations 5 simply offers twenty-two verses, without the use of an alphabet acrostic.

Lamentations 4 also sees the reprisal of 'eka as an opening declaration. The outcry of inexpressible grief represented by 'eka reminds us that we are still confronted with the reality of death. Opening Lamentations 4 with the 'eka after an absence in Lamentations 3 brings us back once more to the necessity of the funeral dirge. Images of death continue to mark the book as Lamentations 4 speaks of bodies in ash heaps (v. 5), dried-up bodies (v. 8), bodies killed by the sword and by famine (v. 9) and the shedding of blood (vv. 13-14). The body of Jerusalem remains in state so the funeral dirge continues.

However, Lamentations 4 is not exclusively a funeral dirge. Actually, the book of Lamentations does not fit neatly into our pre-existing categories. It often blends together different types of lament within the larger genre. Lamentations 3 served mostly as an individual lament, albeit expressed in a communal context with a communal intent. "While chapter 3 can be seen as a portrayal of the exile from the perspective of an individual, chapter 4 focuses on the community and its experience of the siege."[3] Chapter 4 offers a funeral dirge from the perspective of the community and therefore, employs characteristics of a communal lament.

While the funeral dirge reflects on a past event and a set of circumstances (death) that seems irreversible, the communal lament seeks to alter a present set of circumstances or a future event. Nancy Lee describes the key difference between the two forms:

There is a consensus in form critical scholarship (in biblical studies) on the basic difference between these two genres—the dirge and the lament. While both genres deal with the general topic of suffering and loss, the lament prayer (modeled in many psalms) is essentially a *plea* addressed to the deity for intervention for help (thus it is characterized by second person speech). The dirge, on the other hand, *forewarns against* or *commemorates* the fact of a death and/or destruction (and usually employs third person speech).[4]

The two forms overlap in their usage in Lamentations but may hold different motivations and expect different outcomes. Brown and Miller further the distinction between the dirge and the lament.

> The lament prayer is oriented as a plea for help in the terrible moment of suffering and loss, while the dirge, also an act of lamenting, mourns the loss. The lament is often a cry of protest at circumstances of suffering, oppression, and injustice. The dirge, however, can also function in that respect, raising "the voice of public justice" as the "usual 'complaint' about death in the dirge moves to 'accusation' against the perpetrator," the one responsible for the death and destruction.[5]

The dirge of Lamentations 4 can be seen as a form of communal lament placed in the specific context of death. The intention is to offer a public outcry and protest from the community that has suffered and experienced a real death.

Lamentations employs elements of the funeral dirge, the communal lament, the individual lament and the city lament. The intersection of multiple genres yields an expression of lament that is unique because the circumstances surrounding the formation of the book of Lamentations are unique. The forms employed by the author work together to offer a picture of lament that does justice to the overwhelming story of Jerusalem's death and destruction.

Lamentations employs the full range of lament forms to communicate the full range of pain and suffering. Kathleen O'Connor notes that "the poems in Lamentations stretch the lament form to its limits. They reduce or omit features expressing confident hope, assurance, and praise, and they greatly expand the complaints."[6] The genre of Lamentations, therefore, sees the integration of multiple expressions of lament. Each expression offers different layers of suffering that must be unpacked to express the fullness of suffering.

> The terror and incomprehensibility of her situation compels Zion to try to find language within her generic traditions to account for what has happened by countering and navigating the prophetic language that ostensibly already provides a rationale for her experience. The traditional account is no longer tenable in the culmination of what is prophesied. She constructs an alternative story, more authentic to her experience, by drawing on the language of lamentation, combined with elements of city lament and dirge.[7]

Suffering is not to be swept under the rug. Instead, the fullness of suffering is to be declared, with every possible expression at one's disposal.

The dirge elements deepen the sense of loss for the communal lament. "Under the immediate impact of the catastrophe of 587 the collapse of Jerusalem was described in such a way that motifs from the dirge enriched the communal lament. This was because the collapse of the city was experienced as death."[8] Both dirge and lament are at work in the book of Lamentations.[9] The dirge offers the chance to mourn the death of Jerusalem. Lamentation does not state the explicit hope that Jerusalem will be restored, but implicit in the lament genre is the hope that God alone may restore and resurrect Jerusalem.

The prophet-narrator does not back away from the ongoing suffering of Jerusalem. The city has still not experienced restoration, so the lament continues. Lamentations does not offer a quick and easy solution; it continues to offer a snapshot of reality as the listener/reader and even the narrator himself grows weary. O'Connor notes that in Lamentations 4, the shortened acrostic, less personal voice, and absence of address to God convey obliquely what the poem's content presents explicitly. The survivor's strength, emotional responsiveness and capacity to reach for help have shrunk and grown dim like the city's gold (4:1). Resignation and despair have triumphed over anger and resistance. Life recedes and slips away with the ephemeral hope of the previous chapter.[10]

The unfortunate reality is that the circumstances that demanded lament in the first place continue. But Lamentations 4 reminds us to persevere, even as our energy fades. The conditions of suffering persist and so we must persist.

The Ongoing Need for Lament

In the years I have served as an urban pastor and sought to advocate for racial reconciliation and God's justice in the world, there have been too many places of discouragement. Injustice and suffering do not subside. Lamentations 4 keeps coming up even after you've lived through Lamentations 1 and 2. There have been too many tears and too many disappointments. Many years of investment in an at-risk family results, not in a healthy family, but in a more broken family. The youth that the church spent years discipling is sent to jail on gun charges. Friends who give lip service to diversity and racial justice are unwilling to make personal sacrifices for the good of the body of Christ. Colleagues will ask, "What more do you want?" when pleas for racial justice are raised. Sermons on biblical social justice go unheeded as those to whom you preach would rather listen to pundits who derive their rhetoric from their political biases rather than from the Bible.

Even as evangelicals discover and recover these important biblical themes, many want to use these themes to grow their church or expand their influence rather than participate in the enactment of God's justice. The term *justice* is too casually thrown about without the corresponding sacrifice. We want the popularity associated with being justice activists, but we don't want to lament alongside those who suffer. Instead of a justice that arises from the lament of the suffering, justice is misappropriated as a furtherance of the narrative of celebration. American Christian justice leaders are applauded for their self-sacrifice, which allows for a furtherance of Western exceptionalism and even an exploitation of justice as a career-building move. The uplifting of privileged individuals who use justice to expand their own influence serves a narrative of triumphalism rather than engaging the narrative of lament. There are too many examples of justice misappropriated and even thwarted.

It is in those moments that we must bring Lamentations 4 to mind with its complex overlapping of the city lament, funeral dirge and communal lament. Collectively, they offer the voice of the suffering people. It is an act of persistent protest. The fact that the protest continues even after it reaches its peak shows that the wronged will not cease to speak against injustice because injustice persists. Each layer of lament provides a different angle on the story unspooled in the book of Lamentations. The city lament calls us to remember the ongoing pain that is very real on the streets of the city. The funeral dirge calls us to not ignore the painful history. The communal lament reminds us that while sin is personal, it must never be seen as individualistic. The different expressions of lament are offered by a weary voice worn down by the ongoing tragedy, but the lament and the need for lament continue. Even as friends abandon the cause, even as the unrighteous receive favor, even as injustice continues to roll on, the need to cry out in lament does not diminish. Lamentations 4 calls for a faithful persistence in lament, even as the suffering does not dissipate.

THE LUSTROUS TRAP OF CONSUMERISM

Lamentations 4 proceeds to present a series of examples in the city of Jerusalem that reveals how much God's value system differs from our own. He does not respect what we may respect, nor does he desire what we desire. In the first two verses of Lamentations 4, God demonstrates his lack of respect for wealth and material possession by allowing the sacred objects of his temple to be tarnished and stolen.

Verse 1 tells us that the gold has lost its luster, becoming dull, and the sacred gems are scattered. Verse 2 continues that what had once been worth their weight in gold are now pots of clay, a cheap bauble. The material worth of gold and precious stones has now become worthless. The symbol of wealth (gold) is now a symbol of cheapness. A Tiffany diamond has become dollar-store costume jewelry. The use of "three different words for 'gold'"[11] in this text reveals that the decline of wealth in Jerusalem is comprehensive. A contemporary equivalent might state that your checking account and your savings account are bare. Your stocks and bonds are worth less than the paper they are printed on. Your 401k and pension plan have been emptied out. The text reveals that wealth has now become worthless.

In verses 3 and 4, we see Jerusalem long for the security of material possessions. They are unable to feed their young. As the gold has become worthless, they can no longer provide for their children. They now live in material destitution when once they ate delicacies (v. 5). Luxurious purple finery, an object of materialistic desire, now lies in ash heaps (v. 5). Material wealth had provided security and met their excessive desires. Jerusalem's inappropriate longing for gold and their reliance upon wealth as a form of security proved to be misguided desire and trust. God takes those things we hold to be precious apart from him and proves their worthlessness. God does not respect any form of material wealth.

Lamentations 4:1-5 points to the injustice of excessive materialism. The people's misguided dependence on material wealth is challenged in verses 1 and 2. This hope in material wealth is identified as a false hope, as these items are now worthless. The devaluing of wealth in Jerusalem (vv. 1-2) is followed with a description of a heartless people (v. 3) who craved excessive wealth and opulence (v. 5). Jeremiah had warned Israel about the greed of the people and how it would lead to their downfall (Jer 6:13). Yet, they continued to entrust their security to their material wealth, thinking wealth would make everything better. Their craving for wealth has been exposed in Lamentations 4:1-5.

Much like Jerusalem prior to the exile, the American church craves luxury and security. When difficult situations arise and we enter into places of suffering, we revert to base forms of desire and security. In our culture, security is defined by material possessions. The absence of possessions creates great insecurity. But instead of confronting these improper desires, we revert to these dysfunctional desires. Christians face the internal conflict of cultural pressure to seek material wealth in contrast to the scriptural admonition to seek first the kingdom of God.

Christians justifiably reject the materialism of American society. However, Christians are just as susceptible to the trappings of consumerism. In *Consuming Religion*, Vincent Miller examines the pervasiveness of consumer culture in Western society, even in the context of American religion. Our society is consumed by consumerism, and religion is not immune from being co-opted by this dominant ethos. Material culture shapes our worldview with a set of practices that determine our lifestyle.

Patrick Miller probes "how the habits of consumption transform our relationship to the religious beliefs we profess."[12] Consumer culture "is primarily a way of relating to beliefs—a set of habits of interpretation and use—that renders the 'content' of beliefs and values less important."[13] Trips to the supermarket, daily uses of the computer and what we eat and wear are all practices that "form us to think in a way that shows up in our relationship with culture and with religion."[14] In other words, consumer culture has so shaped us that whatever we attempt to live out, even our religious faith, is captive to it.

Consumer culture is able to draw from religious traditions and co-opt what would otherwise be altruistic values to further its own aims. It has the capacity to absorb challenges, even direct challenges to its values. For example, the RED campaign attempted to combat the AIDS pandemic in Africa by asking individuals to purchase as many RED products as possible. $100 million was spent on a marketing campaign to promote increased consumerism in support of combating HIV/AIDS. In the first year, only about $18 million had been raised.[15] The campaign ultimately yielded the most benefit to the companies that garnered positive publicity for their products (as well as increased sales revenue) and to the pharmaceutical companies that increased sales of a product that could have been distributed at a much lower cost. The RED campaign raises the question of whether one can fight injustice while continuing to swim in its waters.

How we seek justice in a materialistic culture may actually result in a deeper commitment to the consumerism of the times. The documentary *Pink Ribbons* reveals that the important cause of breast cancer research has been commodified so that a significant percentage of the funds raised end up in corporate coffers. "Justice" becomes yet another expression of the injustices of consumer culture. Consumer culture is able to devour even the most noble efforts of justice.

Jerusalem was susceptible to the influences of the nations around her. The temptation addressed in Jeremiah 29 revealed how the people of God were tempted to acquiesce to the easy answers and magic formulas offered in Babylon. Israel was often chastised for her captivity to the surrounding culture as evidenced by Lamentations 1. Similarly, evangelical Christianity has the capacity to absorb aspects of the surrounding culture and generate ministry practices that affirm the dominant culture. From George Whitfield's ability to apply the methods of the emerging popular culture of the theater toward evangelistic efforts or Aimee Semple McPherson's ability to tap into celebrity culture, to the latest church growth method that reduces discipleship to a *USA Today*–level of accessibility, evangelicalism has proven to have tremendous capacity for adaptability. This adaptability has led to significant blind spots.

The remnant of Jerusalem also had blind spots. Their very words that speak of their loss of wealth reveal their captivity to materialism. Their improper desire for gold, gems and delicacies reveals a misguided value system. Their connection of wealth to the security and wellbeing of their children further reveals their captivity. YHWH's tearing down of these materialistic systems reveals that he is no respecter of wealth. He has taken these possessions away since they are meaningless. Unfortunately, God's people do not always see things the same way.

In 2010, a major evangelical conference gathered in Cape Town, South Africa. The conference convened Christians from all over the globe and represented the breadth of world Christianity. A notable development for the 2010 gathering was that the majority of the participants originated from the Southern Hemisphere. However, the main leaders and organizers hailed from the European and North American continents.

Reports from Cape Town stressed how many of the speakers proclaimed a deep antipathy toward prosperity theology. Prosperity theology became the whipping boy for this global gathering. Some observers noted, however, that while plenary speakers (mostly from the West) lambasted prosperity theology and excessive materialism, they did so surrounded by high-tech LCD projection, with state-of-the-art audio equipment and a professionally produced, media-friendly product ready for immediate Internet distribution. All of the expressions of conspicuous consumption evident in most American mega-churches were evident but never called into question. It was easy to speak against the injustice of prosperity theology in Africa, but not so easy to stand against the excessive materialism evident in forms of American evangelical Christianity. Consumerism and materialism have so successfully infiltrated American Christianity to the extent that we no longer question or even notice them.

The cultural adaptability of both consumerism and evangelicalism converged in the marketability of justice ministry among young evangelicals in the early part of the twenty-first century. Justice ministry has become a hot commodity among evangelicals, and lucrative careers can now be built on the consumer demands of Christians concerned about justice. All one needs is an unconventional-appearing business card and a website or blog that has heavy Internet traffic in order to become an expert in evangelical justice. Ironically, justice-minded evangelicals expend large amounts of financial resources to consume books, conferences and other sundry consumer products to assuage their guilt over injustice.

Could the newly arrived concern for justice among evangelicals in the twenty-first century actually be a furtherance of consumerism and materialism? In our quest for justice, do we actually contribute to injustice? Many of our expressions of justice may be attempts to package Western guilt and pity in the wrapping paper of compassion. Social justice comes in a box with a clever acronym to sell the product to the American Christian consumer mass market, rather than addressing the actual needs that are voiced by the poor themselves. Because the American church is increasingly captive to the materialistic culture of American society, it is increasingly difficult to speak prophetically against that culture. While there may exist the *rhetoric* of the church against an unjust culture, the *lifestyle* of injustice in the church continues unabated in the context of consumerism.

Lamentations 4 reminds us that material wealth and riches have a greater value to us than they do to YHWH. Even the gold and silver implements in his own temple are easily dismissed. God's people, however, put greater stock on their wealth and riches. Israel saw value in the gold that made up the temple. They were seeing the worth of their temple through the same materialistic lens as the surrounding nations. Their value systems reflected the surrounding culture, so their materialism became acceptable and normative in how they worshiped and lived their lives.

In America, our materialistic endeavors have become acceptable norms. We can validate our excessive materialism by claiming that it is a blessing from God—that we are "blessed to be a blessing"—so our justice endeavors, no matter how materialistic, reflect acceptable norms because they jibe with the end goal of blessing others with our own experiences. We have come to believe that the exceptional American church has the responsibility to bless the world with our success, which may even be a commodified justice that fits the Western world.

Could this inability to move out of the waters of injustice and the quicksand of commodification arise from our lamentable history? Often, texts that critique materialism fail to mention that rampant consumerism may be a product of an American history that viewed life as a consumable. Has sufficient confession been offered in response to the reality that there was a period of American history where there was *actual* commodification of human life, i.e., slavery? How has the act of reducing life to the level of chattel shaped the imagination of modern America? The commodification of human life created the oppressive system of slavery. That system (along with the genocide of Native Americans and the usurping of their land) resulted in great economic growth for the United States over several centuries. The economic engine that arose from these injustices helped to fuel the consumer culture of our current age. As we continue to fuel a system based upon dehumanization and commodification of those made in the image of God, our culpability in racial sin becomes amplified. The practices of a consumer culture, therefore, are not merely economic, they are racially driven. Both consumer culture and American evangelicalism diminish lamentable racial history because the practice of lament over a tainted history would ultimately undermine the existing power structures of both systems.

In *Mirror to the Church*, Emmanuel Katongole examines the tragedy of Rwanda. The genocide in Rwanda occurred in a nation with a high percentage of Christians. Christians slaughtered other Christians.

> Maybe the deepest tragedy of the Rwandan genocide is that Christianity didn't seem to make any difference. Rwandans performed a script that had shaped them more deeply than the biblical story had. Behind the silences of genocide, Hutus and Tutsis alike were shaped by a story that held their imaginations captive.[16]

Katongole recognizes that the Rwandan captivity to the colonial narrative resulted in the failure to embody the Christian narrative in order to combat the ethnocentric narrative of the colonial powers. Captivity to the colonial narrative held greater power than the gospel narrative. Cultural captivity resulted in Rwandans operating under the structures of a racialized narrative over the systems of spiritual redemption and hope.

The blind spots caused by swimming too deeply in society's cultural values may be remedied by offering a radically different set of practices that gesture toward a new reality. Combating injustice may require not only the setting aside of materialistic practices, but the participation in a new set of practices. These new practices must include the practice of lament. Lamentations 4 acknowledges that God's value system regarding wealth differs from the materialism of the world around them. Lamentations 4:6 references Sodom, an extremely negative example, but one that Jerusalem has now become associated with. In Lamentations 4:1-5, those things that had once been beautiful, desirable and a source of their security and strength are now seen as nothing more than common or useless items. God's priorities have won out, and the lamenter must acknowledge this reality.

The acknowledgment of God's value system should result in a shift in practice for God's people. This shift in how we live out faith needs to acknowledge God's priorities in relation to the dominant forms of injustice in our time. The materialistic focus of American Christianity should no longer hold its luster. Lamentations 4 points out the loss of worth of these material possessions and reveals that God's value system greatly differs from our own. God is no respecter of wealth.

A Broken World

Lamentations 4:3-16

Lamentations 4 describes the suffering endured by the weak and innocent: the young (v. 3), the infants and the children (v. 4). Oftentimes, in the midst of suffering, children are the first victims. The impact of the siege is that there is a "lessening of the value of people. . . . Children, considered a blessing and normally valued for their economic contributions to the family and for the family's continuity, become a liability during a siege because they must be fed and cared for."[1] In Lamentations 4, we are confronted with the image of children as extreme victims of the siege. The care of the Jerusalem children is compared unfavorably to how animals care for their children in verse 3. "Zion's children have become worthless, and Zion treats them with even less care than the most despised animals show their offspring."[2] Verse 4 continues this vivid description of suffering children. "Because of thirst the infant's tongue sticks to the roof of its mouth; the children beg for bread, but no one gives it to them" (v. 4). Innocent children suffer the most in a broken world.

The most extreme example of the brutalization of children emerges in verse 10: "With their own hands / compassionate women / have cooked their own children, / who became their food / when my people were destroyed." The horrific image of "compassionate women" doing an unspeakable act causes the listener/reader to recoil at the depths to which the citizens of Jerusalem have fallen. The human standard of compassion and mercy in verse 10 clearly does not merit a positive reaction as they engage in an inhuman act. The community endures great suffering as injustice visits the innocent. The cost of human sinfulness and systemic injustice are evident as the entire community bears the burden. The actions of the community, even the mothers of the children, are considered to be wanting. The consequences of sin have visited the innocent.

Lament over injustice perpetrated on innocent victims reminds us that those most vulnerable—children—are often the first casualties of natural disaster, war or famine. Injustice does not discriminate nor does it offer solace to the innocent. For example, in 2014 at an important juncture in the black lives matter movement, we witnessed the senseless killing of Tamir Rice. The shocking video of a twelve-year-old boy gunned down at a park where he had been skipping around like any other child only minutes earlier challenged our nation to recognize that injustice against black lives is rampant. We lament a broken world where the most vulnerable become victims.

Lamentations 4:5 continues: "Those who once ate delicacies / are destitute in the streets. / Those brought up in royal purple / now lie on ash heaps." The wealthy and the privileged have become destitute and live in squalor. The reversal of fortune for the community reminds the listener/reader that all fall under God's condemnation. Those who have amassed wealth and received honor are not exempt from his judgment.

This revelation should move us to recognize that the world operates under a set of rules and standards different from God's rules and standards. Our perception of righteousness differs from God's standard of righteousness. American Christians tend to define human sinfulness as the active commission of sinful acts, as committing a wrongful act such as stealing or lying, and we identify innocence as those who have not committed these specific acts. Yet defining human sinfulness as simply the commission of particular acts diminishes the central doctrine of the universality of human sinfulness. No one can claim innocence.

God's people are often tempted to engage in relativism when it comes to God's judgment. The go-to excuse for sin is to compare one's own sin to the sins of others. "I may be materialistic but at least I work hard for my money, not like those 'welfare queens' that I hear about." "I sometimes forget to recycle, but the real problem is how China pollutes the atmosphere with their factories." "My uncle is the real racist in the family. Compared to him, my denial of white privilege is not a big deal." But the severity of the sin of others is not the standard by which our own sin is to be judged. Injustice impacts the entire system. The lamenter cries out that human standards are woefully inadequate.

Lamentations 2 established that it is God who brings judgment upon Jerusalem, but the judgment that God brings is a righteous judgment. While some eyes may view these actions as excessive punishment, they are well within the boundaries of God's sovereignty. Our claims of innocence are a form of relativism that diminishes God's call for holiness for all his created beings. We may elevate our own relative sense of innocence, but our human standards of innocence do not absolve us from the breadth of God's righteous judgment.

God's lack of respect for material possessions mirrors God's lack of respect for human status and achievement. A person's status and rank mean nothing before an almighty God. God is the almighty judge, whose actions affect everyone. From one perspective, this type of sovereign power feels overwhelming and potentially unjust. However, the book of Lamentations, culminating in the central verses of Lamentations 3:22-23, consistently reveals a God faithful to his promises and to his covenant. God's integrity stands far above any human standards. His holy character and his immutable promises, rather than the fickle nature of human beings, form the foundation of his actions. He stands far above our expectations of fidelity. Because God's standards so far exceed our own, Lamentations 4 offers several categories that demonstrate that God is no respecter of persons. In the presence of God, we are all equal. We are equal in our disgrace and sin, but ultimately we are equal in how we are loved by God. Lamentations 4, therefore, continues with the devaluing of individuals who may be seen as consecrated before others.

PRINCES, THEN AND NOW

Verse 7 refers to "princes," "consecrated ones" or "Nazirites." The translations offering "princes" or "nobles" could allude to the decline of the ruling class, which would have been adorned with the precious stones mentioned in verse 7. Delbert Hillers counters that "this could be a straightforward reference to Nazirites, that is, men under a special vow to abstain from wine and from contact with the dead, and to let their hair grow long."[3] The decision to translate between "consecrated ones" or "Nazirites" versus "princes" relies on context. In the context of Lamentations 4 where the innocents are subject to judgment, it is reasonable that this lament addresses another sector of society that could be considered innocent or, in this case, consecrated. Nazirites were set aside for a holy purpose in Israel. The most prominent example was Samson, who was known for his long hair and strength, but also for his Nazirite vow (which he repeatedly broke). In some sense, they operate as men with high regard and a high expectation of holiness. The Nazirites were considered the social elite adorned with an aura of consecration who were brought low.

The description of the Nazirites prior to the siege and exile point to the high value placed on these individuals set aside for holy action. Verse 7 colorfully describes the Nazirites as "brighter than snow /

and whiter than milk, / their bodies were more ruddy than rubies, / their appearance like lapis lazuli." The image is not necessarily literal; they were not adorned with jewels, but their appearance was one of brilliance since society upheld their high standing and worth. This colorful, desirable description contrasts to their current reality that "now they are blacker than soot; / they are not recognized in the streets. / Their skin has shriveled on their bones; / it has become as dry as a stick." The healthy image of the Nazirite in verse 7 contrasts to the sickly image in verse 8. Similar to the loss of luster and value in verses 1 and 2, the Nazirites have also lost their luster and worth exemplified by the loss of bright colors. The description of the pious and consecrated Nazirites mirrors the description of the lover in the Song of Songs.[4] This comparison heightens the dramatic decline in their appearance. They go from mirroring the splendor of a bridegroom to a pauper worthy of pity. While Israelite society may have honored the consecrated role of these men, God's standards operate differently. The Nazirites are brought low by the judgment of God.

A possible parallel to the Nazirites in the twenty-first century is our high regard for superstar Christians in American evangelicalism. In lifting up famed pastors and Christian leaders of the twenty-first century, we elevate those we perceive as pious in our American church context. In recent years, we honor younger evangelicals who are engaging in justice ministries or in urban ministry. These types of ministries become a way to elevate ourselves to a whole new level of holiness. We can claim our righteousness by pointing out how much we have given up to serve others.

One contemporary example would be church planters who are moving from the suburbs to the city. Oftentimes, they are white suburbanites who feel called to plant churches in urban, usually inner-city neighborhoods. These relocators become the center of attention among evangelicals. High praise is heaped on the white evangelical church planter for what they have given up. They have left their comfortable suburban existence for the urban context, so we shower them with honor for their self-sacrifice. This emphasis elevates the seemingly pious but often neglects those who have labored in the urban communities for many years. The sense of holiness is conferred on those that have given up so much to live among the poor. But there is no honoring of the poor. After all, the poor have so little to give up. So if the poor remain in their neighborhood to serve their community, then it is not so great a sacrifice—particularly in comparison to the great sacrifice of the affluent suburbanite.

We continue to offer up admiration to the Nazirites of the world who plant urban churches using suburban ministry models. Urban neighborhoods of color are objectified and urban churches of color are diminished. Extant urban churches fail to measure up against the ideal of white suburban churches. Moving from a white suburban neighborhood to a black urban neighborhood is often characterized as a holy act, no matter how short-lived that act may actually be. This act of moving into the urban community fails to recognize the churches that have long served in communities of color.

Many white suburban evangelicals feel called to plant churches in poor black communities. They see this effort as a mission that is necessary to spread the gospel message. These church-planting efforts are seen as the best chance for these poor neighborhoods in desperate need for salvation. Lance Lewis, an African American church planter within an evangelical denomination, comments on the attempt by evangelicals to plant churches in poor black communities:

> The whole premise of evangelicals specifically targeting black people (and, for the most part, dependently poor black people) is, frankly, arrogant. . . . I grew up in a poor black neighborhood . . . and was never more than a block and a half away from a church. I specifically remember hearing the gospel clearly from my grandmother, who was a faithful member of the neigh-

borhood Pentecostal church. Moreover, I distinctly recall the
times my older cousin took me to an evangelistic street outreach.
. . . I remember the night a friend came to take me to National
Temple Church of the Living God, where Bishop Raymond
White was running a revival. . . . He preached the gospel of Christ
crucified and the need for faith in him for forgiveness of sin and
new life. And though the mainstream, dominant culture may be
trending more secular, the same is not true for the majority of
African-Americans. . . . It would be impossible for any evangelical
denomination or ministry to plant a church in an all-black community that doesn't already have several active congregations
serving that community. Since that's true, one must ask the
question: why have we decided to plant here? The unspoken
answer is: the existing black churches just aren't very good.[5]

Instead of supporting the good work already being done in poorer
neighborhoods, white evangelicals insist on starting their own ministries that supposedly have a proven formula for success because
they have worked well in homogenous suburban churches. Indigenous leadership and ministry are considered inferior to the work
of outsiders celebrating their stories of success in the midst of
poverty and suffering. Urban ministry requires both the narrative
of celebration and suffering. By prioritizing ministry methods that
arise from the context of celebration, we lose an important aspect
of the gospel story—redemption that arises out of suffering.

Respecting and honoring the Nazirite confirms the false belief that
if I reach a level of holiness, God will respect me. Despite our primary
gospel conviction that we are saved by grace, many American Christians still operate under the assumption that holiness will find earthly
reward. So American Christians may find ourselves looking for ways
to appear holy. Maybe we look for larger Bibles, degrees from the right
Christian colleges, leadership positions in the church, even religious

tattoos, or maybe we simply try to look the part of a holy person. American Christianity holds to a misguided notion of holiness.

The Nazirites of Lamentations 4 were perceived as holy because of their appearance. Their true holiness, however, did not depend on their appearance. Once God exposes the superficiality of their appearance and the superficiality of Israel's perception of the Nazirites, they are exposed as common, ordinary human beings. They were consecrated because their status was established by God setting them apart for a holy purpose rather than a status that was earned. In American society, our perception of the consecrated ones gravitates toward the beautiful, the wealthy and the powerful. Even if we don't use the word holy to describe these individuals, we treat them as consecrated beings.

Our contemporary descriptions of those we hold in high esteem would mirror the ancient description of the Nazirites in Lamentations 4:7. We value our celebrity pastors because our cultural captivity would consider those who have the appearance of success in our culture (the bestselling authors, the masculine culture warrior, or the urban hipster church planter) as the consecrated. But when we go beyond the surface, don't we find ordinary human beings? God does not respect our human attempts to appear holy and righteous.

The holy and pious are not respected by God, but neither are the kings, prophets and elders. Not even they are exempt from God's judgment. American culture tends to elevate the status of the powerful, whether they are famous athletes, musicians, entertainers or the politically and economically powerful. As a freshman in college I had the opportunity to meet a politician who at that time was considered a potential presidential candidate. Even for a minor national politician, I was in awe. Human power can be an intimidating and intoxicating presence.

Human strength in comparison to God's strength means very little. All the political power in the world does not compare to God's power and authority. If I were to challenge LeBron James or Michael Jordan (in his prime or even way past his prime) to a game of one-on-one, that mismatch would be infinitely less laughable than comparing human power to God's authority. Unfortunately, in an American Christianity built on exceptionalism and triumphalism, we celebrate those who have achieved a certain level of power. I am saddened by Christians who believe God shows his favor by "blessing" certain followers with wealth. We have perpetuated this myth in our culture and our churches by honoring the wealthy, affording them power while simultaneously depriving the poor of opportunity or voice. But this contradicts the message of Lamentations: God is not a respecter of wealth and power. In the New Testament, this assertion is taken even further with the claim that it is easier for a camel to go through the eye of a needle than for someone who is rich to enter the kingdom of God. Our respect for the wealthy and powerful in our society conflicts with the biblical text.

A more subtle expression of American Christianity's obsession with the powerful arises from how the powerful pastor is elevated in contemporary evangelical culture. Radical Christians, hipster Christians, financially successful Christians and even justice-minded Christians can emerge from a consumeristic mindset. White, male, suburban Christians have built megachurches in the suburbs, so they should be the ones we honor. Even more impressive is when they give up their power and wealth to help the less fortunate. Of course, doing good for the very least of these is an important biblical value. However, I am concerned about how a good work that should be done in humility has now become an opportunity to promote the triumphalistic exceptionalism of these ministries. When a megachurch pastor is criticized for spending excessive amounts of money on a home, the justification for the materialism is that much of his income goes to the poor.

The elevation of the powerful, successful pastor is justified by American Christians. The success of that pastor excuses him from acts of ego and hubris—after all, he has earned that right. If that pastor chooses to use church resources to promote his book and extend his financial success, then so be it. The power gained by the pastor is justified by the success of his exceptional ministry. Congregations should follow the successful pastor with full devotion. A prominent megachurch expresses their devotion to their pastor by publishing a document that states: "We serve a Lead Pastor who seeks and hears from God. . . . We serve a Lead Pastor we can trust. . . . We serve a Lead Pastor who pours into us spiritually and professionally. . . . We serve a Lead Pastor who goes first."[6] The document goes on to emphasize the exceptional nature of the lead pastor and the church. Sadly, the name of Jesus is never mentioned once in the thirty points outlined in the document that promotes opportunities to serve the church. The motivation to serve the church is not the example of Christ or the biblical mandate, but rather the charismatic leadership of the lead pastor. This church even offers coloring pages with a picture of the lead pastor with the banner headline: "Unity: we are united under the visionary." How can the culture and ethos of American evangelicalism continue to lift up the powerful, successful, exceptional leaders when Lamentations 4 shows the place of powerful leaders in God's value system?

The hidden narrative of affluent Christians who help others is that we are somehow divinely appointed in some way to be the ones who do the good works. Our motivation may be the elevation of our privilege and our wealth rather than a motivation in the humility of Christ. If we feel that we have been specially anointed because of our success, then our task becomes a dysfunctional dumping of our exceptional cultural values into other communities. There is no sense of mutual learning. An arrogant assumption of unquestioned rightness creeps in to those who see themselves as powerful.

Noted Sri Lankan theologian Vinoth Ramachandra addresses this type of paternalism that assumes the primacy of the American narrative of triumphalism. He writes:

A group of North American pastors calling themselves The Gospel Coalition of International Outreach is engaged in what they call "a mission of Theological Famine Relief for the Global Church." They state on their website: "We are partnering with translators, publishers, and missions networks to provide new access to biblical resources, in digital and physical formats. Our goal is to strengthen thousands of congregations by helping to equip the pastors and elders who are called to shepherd them." Sounds loving, until one asks: who decides who is theologically famished and who is not? who selects what "resources" to send the famished? who decides what constitutes "equipping" and who should be doing it? The answer is always the same. A small group of white, well-to-do American or British males. We have experienced such paternalistic, colonial "mission" before— others deciding what is the "Good News" for us, what is "sound doctrine," which authors to read and whom to avoid, etc. They have exported their theological blind-spots and sectarian rivalries, reproducing carbon-copies of themselves in the global South rather than nurturing real leaders. The learning and theological traffic is all one-way.[7]

The arrogance of the West is the assumption that our forms of piety and power are worth sharing or even imposing. We are obligated to do good works. The challenge to do good works often emerges as: "Do these good works because you have been blessed." Very little consideration is given to the blessings of God already at work. "Go help those pagans with your American capitalistic successes," even if, according to demographics, they are probably already Christians. Our warped sense of what it means to be blessed by God and how we perceive human wealth and power as an earned favor from God results in a dysfunctional view of our worth in God's economy.

Lamentations reminds us that our worth is not based on human values. Lamentations 4 dismantles the wayward cultural values of Israel. What we deem innocent, holy, successful and powerful falls short of the glory of God. Lamentations points out the shortcomings of human efforts and understanding. Those who have been deemed worthy of honor by society are deemed inadequate by God. The consecrated ones with all their adornments are now portrayed in unflattering ways (vv. 7-8). The prophets and the priests, once considered holy, are now seen as blind, defiled with blood and unclean (vv. 13-15). "The priests are shown no honor, the elders no favor" (v. 16). God is not a respecter of our accolades or achievements.

A COMMUNAL LAMENT

In Lamentations 4:17, there is a shift from the third-person perspective to the first. The first-person plural employed reveals the communal element of the lament. Lamentations 4 demonstrates the integration of communal and individual lament. Looking at the book of Lamentations in its entirety, we can also note that the text moves to-and-fro between communal lament and individual lament, such as the transition from the individual voice of Lamentations 3 to the communal voice of Lamentations 4. Lamentations 4:1-16 expresses a communal lament in the third person with a transition to a communal lament expressed in the first-person plural starting in verse 17. Dobbs-Allsopp notes that "the poem shifts into the first-person plural 'we' of the community . . . and the poem's community of readers and hearers is written explicitly into the text."[8] Communal lament draws from the whole community, and a collective voice rises up in lament. The communal lament reveals the impact on the whole community and its response.

Individual lament can also reflect a corporate expression. As we have seen in Lamentations 3, one individual can offer up a personal lament on behalf of the community. By interspersing both types of lament, the distinction between the laments offered on behalf of the community and on behalf of the individual begins to blur. Through both types of lament, individual sin and corporate sin are addressed. Throughout Lamentations, we have encountered various expressions of recognition of corporate sin. In Lamentations 4:17, the first-person plural is used to describe the sin of looking for help other than help from God. "Our eyes failed, / looking in vain for help; / from our towers we watched / for a nation that could not save us" (v. 17). Clearly, the entire city was not perched on the watchtower, but there was corporate culpability in looking for help from another source besides YHWH.

Furthermore, corporate responsibility for corporate sin is evidenced in corporate punishment for sin. Lamentations 4:18 describes this judgment from the first-person plural perspective: "Our end was near, our days were numbered, / for our end had come." Instead of protesting the reality of judgment, there is an acceptance of that reality. O'Connor notes that "unlike the book's other poem's [Lamentations 4] neither speaks to nor petitions God."[9] Berlin notes that "the besieged population waited and waited for help to come from another nation, but none did. Time ran out and the enemy finally entered the city. . . . Second Kings holds out hope for the continuation of the dynasty. Lamentations 4, however, holds out no such hope."[10] There is a resignation to the reality of their judgment.

One of the problems of dealing with corporate sin is the inability to connect individual responsibility for sin with the reality of corporate sin. For example, the easiest way to distance and absolve oneself from the issue of racism is to claim an individual innocence from personal prejudice. For example, the now classic retort "I am not a racist, I have never personally committed a racist act. I have never owned a slave. I have never personally taken land away from a Native American" reduces racism to an abstraction. By reducing racism to purely an individual level, corporate sin is depersonalized and has a higher level of deniability.

The hyperindividualistic tendency of Western culture has determined how we look at the nature of sin. When reading Lamentations 4, the Western reader may be impressed with the depth of individual repentance required in the first part of the chapter. But there is a shift from a first-person individual perspective to a first-person plural perspective in verse 17. A corporate view of sin recognizes the power of sin to impact not only the individual but also the community. In contrast to the corporate lament of Lamentations 4, which acknowledges corporate sin *and* corporate punishment, Western culture prioritizes individual sin *over* corporate sin.

Corporate sin is often denied and dismissed by Western culture's hyperindividualism. This reflects a form of theological liberalism dependent on cultural norms and one's own experience to determine how we understand truth. Sin can be defined by cultural norms and by one's own individual experience. By acquiescing to the cultural norm of hyperindividualism, personal and individual responsibility for structural and corporate sin is denied. The integration of communal lament with individual lament shows the connection between corporate sin requiring communal repentance and individual sin requiring individual repentance. Both forms of lament and repentance are an integral part of Lamentations and the larger biblical witness. Personal and corporate confession is exemplified in Lamentations but also in the corporate laments found in the Psalms, 2 Chronicles 7:14, in the example of Nehemiah, Jeremiah 18:8, in the Gospel of John's use of *cosmos*, and 1 John 1:9.[11]

Lamentations, therefore, does not limit the understanding of human brokenness exclusively to the realm of corporate responsibility or individual responsibility. Both corporate *and* personal expressions are necessary. Communal laments are offered on behalf of the entire community, but never lack a personal expression (see Jeremiah's individual confession on behalf of all of the people of God). In the same way, the expressions of individual lament are not spoken in isolation and do not operate separate from each other. Uniquely expressed individual laments comprise the communal lament of Lamentations.

Through the communal lament the entire community begins to accept the reality of their situation (v. 18). The suffering is personalized as the first-person narration reveals the lament of a defeated people. Their efforts are in vain and they have no choice but to flee or to give in. The community recognizes their downfall and destruction. They see themselves as those who no longer hold a position of honor. They now see that their value systems fall short of God's value system within their city and among their people.

But the final lines of Lamentations 4 point toward one more area where God's value system overrides the human value system. God does not value the great achievement of other cities and nations. The historical and traditional foe of God's people, Edom, wants to gloat over Jerusalem's downfall. "Edom personifies the enemy. . . . Edom is synonymous with Esau, and is thus the symbol of an ancient and perpetual rival to Israel."[12] Edom either sat by idly while their neighbor was conquered, or they may have actually participated in Judah's downfall.[13] But God is not intimidated by Edom, even if Jerusalem is. Verse 21 states: "But to you also the cup will be passed; / you will be drunk and stripped naked." Verse 22 asserts the future judgment of God by stating, "But he will punish your sin, Daughter Edom, / and expose your wickedness." Edom will be judged because God remains the ultimate judge, not just over Jerusalem, but over Edom and eventually over Babylon as well. YHWH's position of authority over all of creation is not challenged, even as Jerusalem crumbles.

DECONSTRUCTING POWER

Throughout the fourth poem, symbols of success and power are deconstructed. Wealth is dismantled (vv. 1-5), consecrated ones are diminished (vv. 7-8), innocence is deconstructed (vv. 3-4, 10), civic leaders are brought low (vv. 13-16), and powerful enemies are exposed (v. 21). American Christians operate under the delusion that success and power provide the answer to the world's problems. In Scripture, we see that powers and principalities are not necessarily a positive expression. Moses stands against the powers and principalities of his time. The prophets boldly speak against the powers, including their own king. Jesus rejects the temptation of secular power. Ephesians 6 portrays powers and principalities as demonic forces. Should we seek the same type of power that the world seeks?

As Christians, we may seek to earn Christian versions of secular power. We often seek to garner respect for ourselves in our chosen world of Christian celebrity. Ministries of justice, racial reconciliation and ministry in the urban context become methods of attaining Christian power and respect. As justice becomes the popular ministry of the moment, more and more evangelicals will use justice ministry as a means of gaining respect. All of us seek some form of respect. We seek respect from our family and friends. We seek respect from our peers and from our society. We are driven to succeed in order to gain this respect. We will earn degrees, accumulate wealth, fight for power. Rather than acquiesce to the world's value system, we should recognize that God dismantles the world's value system.

At this moment after the systematic dismantling of all that the world holds in reverence, we may ask: "What then does God respect? What then does God honor?" We cannot impress God with our past history and our present reality. We cannot impress God with our presumed innocence, piety and power. Prior to Jerusalem's fall, the Israelites had come to see themselves as a special people who had deserved and earned their great city, rather than recognize that everything they had accomplished was by the grace of God. Jerusalem's history is peppered with idolatry and adultery and its reality in exile is one of extreme suffering and misery. In other words, the human achievements of the great city of Jerusalem do not impress God. There is instead the offering of a future hope that "punishment will end" for Daughter Zion. There is a future glory for Zion. But that future glory is based upon the mercies of our God. God is not impressed by what we have done or what we are doing, but instead he honors what he is going to make of us—what *he* does in us and through us.

Lamentations 5

My family currently attends a church where two separate congregations worship together every Sunday. Our church membership is with the multiethnic congregation where fifteen different nationalities are represented in twenty families. Our congregation worships weekly with a Filipino congregation that draws mostly from the Filipino immigrant community in the North Side neighborhood of Chicago. The intersection of these two very distinct congregations on a regular basis has yielded many challenges but also many rewards. The church community offers a rare combination of multiethnic, multicultural, multieconomic class and multigenerational ministry.

In 2013, when one of the most devastating natural disasters struck the Philippines, our two congregations lamented this tragedy together. But it was the Filipino congregation that needed to lead the lament because it was their family members and friends that had been directly impacted by the typhoon. Tears were shed and prayers of lament were offered. It never felt like enough, but room was given to grieve. But what follows lament? Does it end up in a perpetual cycle of tears? We recognized that it would be easy to abruptly stop lament and move on to the next big event as the media was already doing. But the stories of suffering lingered. As the lament was vocalized and prayers were spoken, the tragedy endured. While it is essential that we do not move too quickly from lament, is there a human responsibility once the prayers of lament have been offered?

As the prayers of lament were offered, there was recognition that responsibility could not be absolved. There is great value to lament. Lament must never be cut off before it has run its course, but lament needs a response. That response comes from the Father above, but could it *also* require something from us?

A Lament for Themselves

Lamentations 5

Aftter several chapters of the funeral-dirge genre, we encounter the familiar and recognizable format of the communal lament common to the book of Psalms. Lamentations 4 reflects a myriad of voices that reveals the lament of the community. Lamentations 5 clearly "exhibits the salient features associated with the communal lament."[1] It follows the basic formula and pattern of a typical Hebrew lament: (1) address, (2) complaint, (3) trust (address and praise), (4) address and deliverance. The verses break down into the following:

Verse 1: Address

Verses 2-18: Complaint

Verse 19: Trust (address and praise)

Verses 20-22: Address and Deliverance

By following a familiar format for lament, there is a shift in focus and intent. The elements of the funeral dirge are no longer evident. Delbert Hillers notes that Lamentations 5 "is not written . . . with un-balanced lines, but for the most part in lines where parts balance each other. . . . A higher proportion of synonymous parallelism of a seg-mental type, that is, of the sort where each element in the first half-line is answered by a corresponding element in the second."[2] An imbalanced state of being has been replaced by a more balanced metric presentation. The "all-too-human dirge, which had eyes only for past sorrow and none for God or for any hope for the future, has been scrapped in favor of the format of the lament psalm. The lament psalm is a prayer to God and envisions a potential of renewal and restoration."[3] A hopefulness emerges when this lament prayer is offered by the people of God. The lament offered in Lamentations 5 reflects the perspective of the community as the first-person plural voice dominates. In the first nine verses in particular, we see the communal plea to "Remember, LORD, what has happened to us; . . . see our disgrace" (v. 1). "Our inheritance has been turned over to strangers, / our homes to foreigners" (v. 2). "We are weary. . . . We bear their punishment" (vv. 5, 7). Lamentations 5 presents the collective in a communal lament.

The larger form of communal lament evident in Lamentations 5 also integrates elements of the dialogical lament. Lament not only operates as the place of grieving over suffering, it is also the place of protest. The lament "shifts the calculus and *redresses the distribution of power* between the two parties so that the petitionary party is taken seriously and the God who is addressed is newly engaged in the crisis in a way that puts God at risk."[4] Through the lament, the people talk back to God. "In the Old Testament, from beginning to end, the 'call to distress,' the 'cry out of the depths,' that is, the lament, is an inevitable part of what happens between God and man."[5]

Strangely absent from the book of Lamentations is the voice of God himself. The assertive voice is instead the voice of the suffering. Brueggemann argues that the ability of the author to claim a deep and real suffering is the essence of lament. The lament expressed in a worship setting gives voice to the sufferer. "The basis for the conclusion that the petitioner is taken seriously and legitimately granted power in the relation is that the speech of the petitioner is heard, valued and transmitted as serious speech. Cultically, we may assume that such speech is taken seriously by God."[6] The worship life of Israel took seriously the role of lament. In contrast, the worship life of American evangelical Christianity is often devoid of lament. We ignore a key expression of worship and prayer and the opportunity to speak to God out of the midst of suffering.

The legitimation of the voice of the suffering offers the very real possibility of justice being called out. Nancy Lee finds this power in the dirge. "The dirge serves a formal social function in a community by raising 'the voice of public justice' . . . when the dirge or funeral singer identifies and accuses the murderer who caused a death."[7] For Brueggemann, the power of the lament is that the oppressed are given the right to speak and, by speaking, offered the possibility of re-dressing injustice. "The lament form thus concerns a redistribution of power."[8] The power of lament is that the covenant relationship op-erates in both directions: from the powerful to the powerless as well as from the powerless to the powerful. Lament offers a mutual dy-namic to the covenant relationship. "One loss that results from the absence of lament is the loss of *genuine covenant interaction*, since the second party to the covenant (the petitioner) has become voiceless or has a voice that is permitted to speak only praise and doxology."[9]

Lamentations, therefore, offers the example of the lesser party in the covenant talking back to the greater party in the covenant through lament. God is silent, but not absent. Lament is the opportunity for the suffering to speak. "In the West, God-talk is characterized by objective thinking about God. In theology God becomes an object. But in the Old Testament, talk of God is characterized by dialogical thinking."[10] Lament creates space for this dialogue and moves the theology of suffering into interaction with the theology of celebration.

A theology of celebration has the luxury of being able to objectify God, and because suffering is kept at a distance it is not necessary for the presence of God to be immanent. God can be a distant abstraction whose praise is expected. For example, Westermann notes that

when Western theology speaks of God's salvation or of a God
who saves, God thereby becomes objectively tied to an event,
and thus emerges a "soteriology." The Old Testament cannot
pin God down to a single soteriology. It can only speak of God's
saving acts within a whole series of events, and that necessarily
involves some kind of verbal exchange between God and man.[11]

Lament as dialogue challenges the notion of an abstract relationship with God. A theology of suffering must acknowledge the
cry of distress and suffering in lament before moving to the psalms
of praise. Lamentations presents an example of staying in the dialogue of lament as those who suffer offer the relentless truth about
suffering. Dialogical lament becomes a form of prayer.

"It has taken a long time, but now the community is ready to take
over for itself those modeling, prayer-centered efforts."[12] Laments
that have described suffering in no uncertain terms in the earlier
chapters now more intentionally offer prayers that petition God,
while remaining in the larger genre of lament as a dialogical lament.
There is the prayer for YHWH to "remember," to "look" and to "see"
(v. 1). Lamentations moves toward a direct petition that honors God
with "You, LORD, reign forever; / your throne endures from generation to generation" (v. 19). This statement is followed by a questioning plea: "Why do you always forget us? / Why do you forsake us
so long?" (v. 20). The prayer concludes with a direct plea: "Restore us
to yourself, LORD, that we may return; renew our days as of old" (v.
21). As lament is offered throughout the book of Lamentations and
moves into dialogical lament in the final chapter, the final movement
is toward a direct prayer of help offered to God.

Personified Jerusalem has expressed the people's experience and
the prophet-narrator has spoken on their behalf, but now the people
pray for themselves and speak to God for themselves. In many of our
justice endeavors, we often believe that our task is to speak for the

voiceless. But maybe we need to follow the book of Lamentations and move the ones who suffer to front and center. The prophet-narrator has much to say, but the real movement and progress is that we hear the actual voice of those who suffer. The people pray for themselves. Oftentimes, in corporate prayer meetings, we offer prayers on behalf of the suffering; even when an individual is present, that individual remains silent while others pray. The example of Lamentations may be to move those who suffer to exercise the dignity of human agency and become empowered to pray for themselves.

The movement from an advocate speaking on behalf of others to the sufferers speaking up for themselves offers hope to all who suffer.

> Where there is lament, the believer is able to take initiative with God and so develop over against God the ego-strength that is necessary for responsible faith. But where the capacity to initiate lament is absent, one is left only with praise and doxology. God then is omnipotent, always to be praised. The believer is nothing, and can praise or accept guilt uncritically where life with God does not function properly. The outcome is a "False Self," bad faith that is based in fear and guilt and lived out as resentful or self-deceptive works of righteousness. The absence of lament makes a religion of coercive obedience the only possibility.[13]

The speaking of lament by those who suffer presents a new stage for the book of Lamentations.

Part of the important work in ministries of justice for the marginalized is the empowering of those who suffer to find their voice. The power of the prophet-narrator to speak on behalf of those who suffer is an important development for ministries of justice. However, these empathic expressions on behalf of the other are not an end in themselves. The movement of Lamentations is toward those who suffer speaking for themselves. Luke Bretherton argues that "a church is constituted as a public body through listening to both God and the strangers among whom it lives."[14] I would add that part of Christian witness is to empower the other to express to God and to the public body the truth of a story that has long remained hidden. How are the suffering narratives of the African American community embraced rather than shunned? Can the stories of black victims of terrorist violence (such as the African victims of Boko Haram) be just as important a prayer topic as the victims of terrorist violence in France? In our sermon illustrations, are we willing to share about the successful mission efforts of George Liele and not just quote from the meanderings of a megachurch pastor? The narrative of triumph has taken center stage in our church. Can we elevate these hidden stories in what we teach in our seminaries, in our denominations and in our church life?

REMEMBER GOD

Lamentations 5 begins with a direct address by the people to God. The opening invocation directly addresses God to "remember" or to "consider," and to "look" or "pay attention," and to "see" in order to draw attention to Jerusalem's state (v. 1). O'Connor notes that "the request for God to remember, new in this book, involves more than intellectual recall of past events. . . . It calls God to bring their suffering alive and to reenter it in the present. . . . It is imperative that God brings their suffering into consciousness."[15] The opening cry, for God to remember, gestures toward the possibility of hope. As the people pray to God, they plead for God to remember their suffering in context of the covenant. Having established the covenant loyalty of God in Lamentations 3, God's people now have recourse. This last poem once again acknowledges that the source of all mercy and hope is YHWH.

If we are to acknowledge the full power of God, we must remember that God's covenant is at work on behalf of his people. This passage recognizes that God is the God of history and that he is in charge. The sovereign God of history did not make a mistake. When

God makes a covenant, he remains loyal and faithful to that covenant. The hope of Lamentations arises from reliance upon God's mercy. This hope leads God's people to lift up this prayer in Lamentations 5. The belief that God is the ultimate judge allows the community to lay bare, once more, their story of suffering and pray an honest prayer of lament.

After the initial plea, the communal voice draws attention to the crumbling family structure evident in their community. "We have become fatherless, / our mothers are widows" (v. 3). "Verses 2-3 show a progression from inherited land to household to father (head of household). . . . The most basic elements of the social structure—the family unit and the mechanism for preserving its continuity through inheritance—have been wiped out."[16] The lament of Lamentations 5:2-3 reflects the deep sense of insecurity brought upon them. This loss resulting from the crumbling family system leads to the daily struggle for survival. Basic, everyday necessities that should be readily available, such as water and wood (v. 4), become scarce. They are in a constant state of pursuit without any rest (v. 5).

The pressures of material survival are exacerbated by an intense suffering manifest in physiological and psychological effects.[17] Verses 7 to 10 describe the pain of punishment (v. 7), slavery and the lack of freedom (v. 8), a constant sense of risk and danger (v. 9), and the pain of starvation (v. 10). Their suffering is not only physical, but also shapes their psychological well-being as they live under the constant burden of survival. A theology of suffering profoundly shapes their community's worldview and perspective.

The recapitulation continues with further description of brutality against Jerusalem's population, including sexual assault and physical violence (vv. 11-14). This section revisits the various citizens of Jerusalem including women, virgins (young women), princes, elders, young men and boys to hear their stories of suffering. The populace has endured various public indignities and trauma, but each individual story contributes to the power of the communal lament. The complaint closes with the downfall of the public institutions and the decline of the civic domain as "the elders are gone from the city gate" (v. 14), which references the loss of the judicial system. Celebratory worship characterized by music and dancing has ceased (vv. 14-15). Their place of worship has also been destroyed: "Mount Zion, which lies desolate" (v. 18). The civic authority, the crown, is also gone. From family systems to public institutions, every aspect of life has been destroyed, leading to the appropriate complaint by the community.

The prolonged complaint section of this lament points to the level of desperation experienced by God's people and recapitulates the depth of suffering that is the story throughout the book of Lamentations. The community now offers up a prayer that speaks honest truth about their condition. In a moment of great despair, God's people cry out in a prayer of lament. The extended complaint section reminds us once more that our prayers are often triumphalistic. We're ready to ask for the next big item that is due us, and we pray prayers that will get that item of blessing that we think we deserve. We will pray for bigger churches, larger budgets, slimmer waistlines, more purpose in our lives, but we do not pray in recognition of the deepest suffering in our own lives or in the lives of others. Our prayers border on idolatry where we expect vending-machine type of results. Verses 2 to 18 remind us that there is suffering in our community and that suffering is worth hearing. Lament is often the appropriate response for our current situation.

In the work of urban ministry, justice ministry and racial justice ministry, there is the strong temptation to claim victory: we have fixed our neighborhoods, we have raised a million dollars or we now have black friends. We can go through the whole litany of our accomplishments and claim victory over injustice. Lamentations 5 is a stark reminder that suffering is not a passing condition that provides a mere bump in the road toward celebration. We must plumb its depths.

Furthermore, the recapitulation of suffering has a direction and purpose. It once again draws attention to the one who can hear and act upon our suffering. In my spiritual journey, I have been blessed by African American and Native American leaders who have spoken great wisdom to my life, marriage and ministry. Their lives present a testimony of deep suffering that has marked their communities for generations. Their stories reflect the historical and ongoing suffering of their communities. Even in the expression of the breadth of their suffering, I find great hope. Suffering is not glossed over but embraced as a necessary part of worship. The gospel music of the African American church tradition speaks about the reality of suffering, ultimately offering hope:

Precious Lord, take my hand
Lead me on, let me stand
I am tired, I am weak, I am worn
Through the storm, through the night
Lead me on to the light
Take my hand, precious Lord, lead me home

When my way grows drear
Precious Lord linger near
When my life is almost gone
Hear my cry, hear my call
Hold my hand lest I fall
Take my hand, precious Lord, lead me home

When the darkness appears
And the night draws near
And the day is past and gone
At the river I stand
Guide my feet, hold my hand
Take my hand, precious Lord, lead me home

Precious Lord, take my hand
Lead me on, let me stand
I am tired, I am weak, I am worn
Through the storm, through the night
Lead me on to the light
Take my hand, precious Lord, lead me home[18]

IS THERE HOPE FOR THE CITY?

Lamentations 5 speaks of the loss of the inheritance given to Israel by God (v. 2). That inheritance is Jerusalem herself, which has been destroyed with many of her citizens sent into exile. Drawing upon the themes outlined in the first four chapters, the communal lament of Lamentations 5 once again highlights Jerusalem's destruction. Because Jerusalem's once high standing has been brought low, a pessimist (or a realist) could deduce that God is now gone from the midst of his people. Dobbs-Allsopp notes that

> the way city laments typically end brings Lamentations' conclusion more sharply into relief. . . . The Mesopotamian city laments usually end by depicting the return of the gods and the ensuing restoration of the city. . . . What follows in Lamentations 5 is not a description of a restored Jerusalem in which God will once again take up residence, but yet another rehearsal of Jerusalem's destruction.[19]

God's departure from the city is evidenced by Jerusalem's destruction but also the absence of worship in the conquered city: Mount Zion is desolate and worship has ceased. "Verse 18 makes explicit what was implicit in the preceding verses, namely, that the temple is destroyed."[20] The temple of YHWH is a victim of the conquest, and there is no longer a temple to house his special presence so that he can be worshiped in Jerusalem.

Lamentations 5:19, however, moves toward a hopeful note for

God's people and the city. The fifth poem concludes with a direct address to God. Verse 19 offers an expression of praise to YHWH, albeit a relatively brief statement. "You, LORD, reign forever; / your throne endures from generation to generation." The use of the "you" at the beginning of the Hebrew sentence may indicate emphasis. I agree with O'Connor, who sees the pronoun here as "an attention-getting device, an emphatic appeal to awaken God's notice and to make a personal connection with God, as if to say, 'You, YHWH, no one else, only you.'"[21] The community recognizes the uniqueness of God in their appeal to God. In Mesopotamian city laments, deities are localized and dwell only in their designated cities. YHWH, however, transcends a specific location. God can restore Jerusalem even without a house of worship for himself in Jerusalem.

Verse 19 affirms that God endures beyond the limitations of Jerusalem. Even in the absence of the temple in Jerusalem and even with Mount Zion laid waste (v. 18), YHWH remains enthroned and reigns over all. "God is not physically or spatially limited to his temple, and his existence does not depend on a physical structure."[22] God's people have the hope and assurance that they worship a God who is not limited by human boundaries. Unlike the gods of the times, God is not bound to one city or one location.

Israel's prayer acknowledges that the restoration of the community can only come through a restored relationship with God. Because God remains on the throne from generation to generation, hope comes in God's remembrance (v. 1) and that God will not forget nor forsake (v. 20). The restoration longed for in Lamentations 5:21 requires reconciliation with YHWH. This possibility is not merely the restoration of Jerusalem as a city, but hope in the power of God's eternal reign. Restoration will occur according to God's sovereign plan, but it may not be what the Israelites desire. Their expectation that God will restore Jerusalem to its former glory is not what actually happens.

Even after the temple is rebuilt at a later date from Lamentations, the people continue to lament. Haggai 2 points out the deficiency of the reconstructed temple by asking, "Who of you is left who saw this house in its former glory? How does it look to you now? Does it not seem to you like nothing?" (Hag 2:3). The reconstructed temple left much to be desired in comparison to the glory of the temple built by Solomon. But unexpectedly, Haggai affirms the glory of the new temple. He claims: "'The glory of this present house will be greater than the glory of the former house,' says the LORD Almighty. 'And in this place I will grant peace,' declares the LORD Almighty" (Hag 2:9). The glory of the present house (the reconstructed temple) is made glorious by the arrival of "what is desired by all nations" (v. 7). The hope expressed in Lamentations will be fulfilled not in the restoration of Jerusalem to its former glory but will be evidenced by a new glory. Lamentations 5 reveals a devastated Jerusalem without a temple. But YHWH transcends the limitations of geography. Restoration will come in the person of Jesus, who "is desired by all nations." A new hope arises from Jerusalem in the person of Christ. Restoration of Jerusalem will not occur in the manner that is anticipated by the remnant in Jerusalem, but God's sovereign provision, which is not limited by time, space and human design, will occur in accordance to his sovereign plan.

When white evangelicals abandoned the city in the twentieth century and fled to the suburbs, many assumed that the presence of God had also fled the city. The modern city was seen as devoid of God's presence. There was an assumption that new Jerusalems were being established in the suburbs with the concomitant building of new and impressive houses of worship. In time, the narrative of a city without hope became a part of the modern-day evangelical vernacular. Modern-day evangelicals look upon the city with the assumption that the city is spiritually dead. As outlined earlier, twentieth-century evangelicals began to weave a narrative of distrust and suspicion of the city. The abandonment of the city by twentieth-century evangelicals distanced them from the stories of the "have-nots" and other suffering communities. Instead of finding YHWH still indwelling the city, American evangelicals engaged in a bodily passivity and disconnect in the safe confines of suburban life.

Lamentations 5 reveals God as enthroned above and beyond the strictures of the city. YHWH is transcendent and not limited by an earthly container. Even if we were to abandon the city and lose the structures that made our faith work, God remains Lord over the city. God is in charge of the restoration.

In *Flesh and Stone*, Richard Sennett examines the evolving view of the city over the course of human history and attempts to present a "history of the city told through people's bodily experience." Sennett suggests that the self-perception and understanding of the human body ultimately shapes how we view the city, even in how we design and build our cities. The city, therefore, becomes an extension of the human body. It is a material reality based upon the material reality of human flesh. Additionally, from Sennett's perspective, the modern city is a passive body. Passive human bodies compose the passive body of the city. How does the human body already wrapped up in passivity interact with the city made passive by the passive bodies that compose it? The key question for Sennett, therefore, is "how do we exit our bodily passivity?"[23]

Our inquiry into the nature of the church in the urban context examines how the body of Christ can relate to the body of the city. If indeed the key characteristics of the modern body and the modern city are the passive body and the passive city, how do we respond as the body of Christ in the face of such passivity? If the physical reality of the body of the city must be confronted with another physical reality then the bodily passivity of the city must be contrasted by the active body of Christ: *the church*. However, is the body of Christ also a victim of this passivity? Is the body of Christ even more susceptible to this form of bodily passivity, resulting in the disempowerment of the church?

Sennett's sociological question becomes the key theological question for ministry in the urban context. How does the body of Christ, the church, move from bodily passivity to body *activity*? This activity does not necessitate a certain type of political action, but it does involve the commitment to move toward the actual embodiment of Christ in the world. Without compromising the specific calling of the church, how do we understand an active body of Christ as it interacts with the body of the city? If the perception of the human body shapes the body of the city, then the way the church understands itself as the embodiment of Christ should transform our interaction with the body of the city.

Our understanding of the incarnation, therefore, takes on an added measure of importance. In the incarnation, there is the full expression of God's active love for humanity and the act of making his dwelling among us. The incarnation, therefore, gives us the model of an active body of Christ confronting the passive body of the city. Since the city is a material reality (albeit with certain characteristics of passivity), the material reality of the body of Christ, the church, operates as the expression of God's activity in the city.

In Lamentations 5, we observe a God who operates beyond human limitations and expectations; his act of restoring is not limited to how the idols of the world operate. The passivity of the urban body contrasts to the active work of God's body as initially expressed through the person of Jesus. Lamentations longs for the restoration of Jerusalem, but Lamentations 5 reminds the community that restoration is in the hands of God. God will indeed make his dwelling among them. However, that indwelling is not ultimately tied to a building but rather to the presence of God in Christ.

The theological narrative of the incarnation can provide the motivation and paradigm of ministry for the body of Christ in the context of the city. The role, value and contribution of the church in the city could be defined by her identity as the embodiment of Christ. As Sam Wells states,

> What if the Church were seen not as a means to an end, but an end in itself? What if the basis of Christian life were, as for Paul in 1 Corinthians, what will build up in the Church? . . . Could it really be that the Church is not an embarrassing witness to Christ, a paltry imitation of the perfect interdependence of the Trinity, but indeed the body of Christ, the very human but also divine image of God on earth?[24]

As the biblical motif suggests, the church as the body of Christ is both the human and divine embodiment of Christ. Determining the role of the church requires an understanding of the connection between the incarnation of the body of Jesus in the world and the incarnation of the body of Christ in the city.

Lamentations 5 reveals that God reigns, even in the absence of an earthly temple. God transcends human limitations. However, the hope for restoration comes not from a distant God but from Immanuel, "God is with us." The sovereign God who provides hope for Jerusalem also provides a physical human body in the person of Christ, incarnate in our world. The church as the body of Christ now embodies Christ in the world. The bodily passivity of an abstract and distant God is not allowed for those who live in the material reality of the city. The church is called to embody Christ in the city.

ENDING IN A MINOR KEY

The book of Lamentations ends in a minor key. Musical pieces that end in a minor key often signal that issues have not quite been resolved—they leave you hanging. The book is an unfinished story. There is no clear-cut resolution in Lamentations. The answer is not quite clear because there is no triumphant return to Jerusalem by the end of the book. There is no immediate and clear victory brought about by Israel's warriors. No easy answer is offered. The answer will come later.

One application of the open-endedness of the book of Lamentations is found in how modern Jews read their own history. The commemoration of the Tisha B'Av connects the ancient history of the fall of Jerusalem in 586 B.C. to the second fall of Jerusalem in A.D. 70, then ultimately to the Holocaust of the twentieth century. History and the impact of history are ongoing. This perspective is practiced in the breaking of glass at Jewish weddings, which reminds the community of the destruction of the temple. Leaving a small corner of the Jewish house unpainted reminds them that their personal house should not be finished while the temple of YHWH remains in ruins. The historical narrative is not left in an abstracted and distant form. Instead, it is a pervasive story that remains a part of the everyday life of the believer.

From the climax of the acrostic structure in Lamentations 3, the book moves in a downward slope. The final chapter therefore offers a recapitulation of the major themes and closes seemingly without a major resolution. The final verse states, "Unless you have utterly rejected us / and are angry with us beyond measure." The narrative remains unresolved; a quick and easy solution is not offered. Hope is deferred, but it is not absent. The closing of the book on a minor note opens the possibility of the resolution coming at a later point in history.

Hope for the exiles is found in the Old Testament in the latter chapters of Isaiah. Isaiah 40 begins with "Comfort, comfort my people, / says your God. / Speak tenderly to Jerusalem, / and proclaim to her / that her hard service has been completed," which offers the comfort that was absent in the first chapter of Lamentations. Isaiah 49:8 offers the hope of restoration, but only in God's timing. "In the time of my favor I will answer you, / and in the day of salvation I will help you." God is not silent in offering the hope of salvation. Isaiah 52 expands on this hope with a call to "Awake, awake, Zion, / clothe yourself with strength! . . . The uncircumcised and defiled / will not enter you again. . . . Free yourself from the chains on your neck, / Daughter Zion, now a captive" (vv. 1-2). Freedom is coming for God's people. This freedom, however, is not simply the restoration of Jerusalem and a return to the Promised Land. Beginning with Isaiah 52:7, we discover that there is good news. However, this news does not focus on material gain or political power, but instead it is the good news that God reigns.

The good news found in the prophets is not simply that Jerusalem will be restored, but that God will restore and renew a *relationship* with his people (Lam 5:21). This good news connects us to the expression of the good news in the New Testament: the gospel of Jesus Christ. That relationship of God with his people will take a new form since his reign will not continue through a political king on the throne in Jerusalem, but through the fulfillment of the hope of restoration through the person of Jesus.

The reign of God will continue through Jesus. The close of Isaiah 52 begins the section describing the suffering servant. Isaiah 52:14 describes the suffering servant with an appearance "so disfigured beyond that of any human being / and his form marred beyond human likeness." Isaiah 53:2-3 continues the description: "He had no beauty or majesty to attract us to him, / nothing in his appearance that we should desire him. / He was despised and rejected by mankind, / a man of suffering, and familiar with pain. / Like one from whom people hide their faces / he was despised, and we held him in low esteem."

The good news of the reign of God does not begin with a triumphant military victory by an exceptional hero, but instead the good news of the reign of God is connected to a "have-not." A *suffering* servant. The other. The Messiah "took up our pain / and bore our suffering. . . . He was pierced for our transgressions, / he was crushed for our iniquities" (Is 53:4-5). Our Messiah's identity, therefore, is not based upon his assertion of power, but the humility of his suffering. The resolution for Lamentations is deferred until the fulfillment that occurs in the New Testament. The unusual answer comes in the person of Jesus who resolves the narrative of Lamentations. The story of Lamentations is completed in the incarnate Jesus who comes to dwell among human flesh in the body of the city.

Christology plays a central role in the resolution of the themes in Lamentations. Since Jesus is the answer to the questions in Lamentations, Jesus must be understood well to understand those answers. Therefore, Christology needs to be shaped as much by lament as by praise. Otherwise, the theology of celebration overwhelms the theology of suffering and we have an imbalance and dysfunction. Lamentations helps us correct the imbalance with the narrative of suffering.

The answer of Jesus requires the full testimony of Scripture. Lamentations offers a realistic snapshot of a fallen city, then moves toward the acceptance of this suffering reality and finally turns to YHWH for salvation. Lamentations, therefore, serves to correct a triumphalistic worldview that seeks to fix the problems of the world through human effort. A warped theology of celebration elevates human effort and ultimately undermines a robust Christology. If Jesus is not properly understood in the fullness of lament and praise, then a dysfunctional Christology only exacerbates the problems encountered in Lamentations.

True Incarnation

One of the expressions of a dysfunctional Christology is a dysfunctional understanding of the incarnation. Incarnation can be co-opted by those who live under the theology of celebration and misapplied to offer inadequate answers to the questions raised by Lamentations. A modern Western worldview tends toward abstraction in theological engagement, so seeing Jesus exclusively through this abstracted lens allows individuals to cast themselves in place of the divine Jesus. We place ourselves in the position of deity. We seek to be like Jesus in his heroic work of incarnation.

Incarnation has been used as a key motif in urban and justice ministry. Unfortunately, a powerful doctrine has been recast and misapplied, allowing the dysfunctional narrative that elevates the ministry approach and systems of white evangelicals over and above those in minority communities. Incarnational ministry has frequently come to mean the relocation of the educated, affluent, white suburbanite to help the poor, black urbanite. White Christians empty themselves of the blessings of their suburban existence and humble themselves to save poor folks in the city.

The recent surging interest in urban ministry, particularly in urban church planting, is a notable development in American Christianity. The narrative of an affluent, privileged individual or community moving into the poor neighborhood has become a prominent motif for evangelical Christians. Incarnational ministry as defined by American evangelicals can abstract and romanticize both the city and the role of the church in the city: the city is idealized as a place of great need, and the pastor or community that relocates to the city takes on the idealized role of Christ in the city.

When I meet new urban church planters who are relocators, many do not necessarily feel called to a specific neighborhood. Their call to the city is not based upon a deep God-given burden for a community that they have lived in for decades. Instead, the abstracted city becomes a testing ground for ministry models and paradigms that have worked well in white, suburban neighborhoods. Doing ministry *for* the urban community may become central, more than doing ministry *with* the people of the neighborhood.

Incarnational ministry as a concept becomes problematic in its abstracted application. The theology can be easily misapplied when abstracted beyond the specific biblical expression for the incarnation. Applying the incarnation narrative to the urban church requires the recognition of key limitations. One of the most significant potential misapplications of the concept of incarnational ministry in the urban context is thinking that in every way the church can mirror the power and mystery of Christ's incarnation. But a key to true incarnational life of the church in the city requires the awareness that the church is *not* the complete and perfect reflection of Jesus' incarnation. While the church is established by Jesus as a holy institution, it is still comprised of human beings with human limitations. The church's imitation of Christ should not be seen as a strict one-to-one correspondence between the incarnation of Jesus and the embodiment of Christ in the city through the church.

In 2010, two movies explored the theme of relationships built across cultural division. James Cameron's *Avatar* created an animated world rich in visual detail and filled with "realistic" images and scenes. The story, however, was somewhat formulaic. Boy looks for a new life. Boy meets girl. Boy loses girl. Boy saves the girl's entire species. The lessons in the movie were a bit ham-handed. Climate care and no war for oil were clear political messages made by the movie. However, these points were made while exoticizing native cultures. The images of the Na'vi (Na'vi = Natives) riding on horseback with bows and arrows and loud war cries could not have been more obvious. Of course, that charge was led by the John Wayne-ish white male.

That same year saw the release of *The Blind Side*, a true story about a black football player adopted by a white family. The movie portrayed Christians in a positive light with the rich private school accepting the poor black kid because it was their Christian responsibility. And it was very noble of the rich white family to take in the poor black kid because of their good Christian nature. The family rescues the homeless black kid—one child at a time brought into Noah's Ark out of the waters of judgment.

The two movies took different approaches to saving the other. *Avatar* upends the system and *The Blind Side* saves the individual. In both movies, however, you have white heroes rescuing the minorities. In *Avatar*, it was made clear that the natives were not going to win without the messianic leadership and superior flying abilities of the white male hero. In *The Blind Side*, it was pretty evident that the young black man would not have found success without the help of the white family.

There were strongly redemptive elements in both movies, but when do we start seeing all the different groups working together rather than the white person rescuing the minority person? *Avatar* seems to advocate for the incarnational model of ministry, while *The Blind Side* seems to advocate for the rescue-mission model of ministry. Whichever model is used, both models require the heroic white American.

A few years ago I was speaking at a mission conference comprising mainly white suburbanite participants. I was listening to the speaker before me, when he dropped this little gem: "It's not about a handout, but a hand up." Actually, it's not about either. A handout means you think you're better than me and you're handing me something (something I probably don't deserve). A hand up means you think you're better than me and you're trying to lift me up from a bad place to your wonderful place. Actually, if it's a choice between the two, I'd rather have the handout. If you're going to be condescending, I might as well get a direct benefit out of it instead of being told that I need to become like you. Forget the handout or the hand up. Just reach a hand across. Let's be equals and partners. I don't need you to rescue me, just like you don't think you need rescuing by me. My rescuer is a Jewish carpenter. I want to be a colaborer in Christ with you, not your reclamation project.

The open-ended conclusion of Lamentations points us toward the answer found in the book of Isaiah and in the Gospels. The incarnation of Christ provides the hope for Christians. Despite the overwhelming emotions of the book of Lamentations, trust in YHWH as deliverer offers the answer to the challenges raised by the text. For Christians, Lamentations gestures toward the work of Christ, not of human effort to restore and to heal. However, if viewed through a warped Western framework of triumphalism and exceptionalism, the answer to Lamentations becomes the successful, suburban, white male hero. But instead, the lingering question of Lamentations 5:22 needs to be answered by the life of Jesus embodied in the community of believers.

CAN THIS DEAD BODY LIVE?

Lamentations closes with a final plea for restoration. The people of God long for renewal, reconciliation and restoration. This plea, however, arises from the recognition that God is in control. Only by the grace of God is hope reintroduced to God's people. American exceptionalism embraces a work-centered soteriology, believing that the United States of America has earned a special status before God, attaining favor through her exceptional actions. This assumption stands in stark contrast to the humility and dependence on God revealed in the book of Lamentations. Lamentations call us to return to a renewed sense of hope, not in our own strength but in God's provision.

Lamentations 5 pleads for a renewal that depends on God's mercy. Revival is a high value among American evangelicals. Some Christian colleges hold mandatory revivals on a yearly basis. Historically, renewal movements arose out of a deep humility that acknowledged human dependence on God because renewal is dependent on God. However, most of our revivals seem to rely on prescribed playbooks to foment revival, magic formulas to set the stage for revival. Dimmed lights, loud music and preaching that causes cognitive dissonance, followed by music that tugs at the heartstrings and plants placed in the audience are a few of the methods used to spark revival at Christian gatherings.

Lamentations 5:1 calls upon God to "remember." After an entire book of remembering and lamenting, my personal desire at this point is to bring the lament to a halt and to move toward restoration. Remembering has been a painful exercise so far, but this call to remembrance is not a furthering of a pity party. It is instead a call for God to remember, to take heart, consider, look, see and ultimately to act on their behalf. Even as God's people lament and draw attention to their suffering, this act reflects the realization that God is the only hope. But hope will only arise if God remembers. Human effort will not restore Jerusalem to its former glory nor will it restore the glory of any city. Instead, it is the sacrifice of the body of Christ that brings complete healing.

Conclusion

Lamentations provides a necessary corrective to the triumphalism and exceptionalism of the American evangelical church arising from an ignorance of a tainted history. This creates theological dysfunction exacerbated by the absence of lament. The counternarrative to a culturally captive narrative has been silenced with the absence of lament.

To counter these trends, the practice of lament must be purposely reintroduced to the church. How are American evangelicals practicing the opposite of lament and developing habits that further triumphalism and exceptionalism? How can the church reverse the trend and offer counteracting practices? As Sam Wells points out, "Repeated practice nurtures skill, an excellence that derives from repeated performance. Skill develops habit, a disposition to use skills on occasions and in locations different from the times and places where the skill was developed. Habit develops instinct, a pattern of unconscious behavior that reveals a deep element of character."[1] We must engage in practices that form habits and instincts that differ markedly from the current practices of dysfunctional Christianity.

Can our worship practices begin to change? We could begin with more integration of lament and the book of Lamentations itself into our liturgy, our worship songs and our preaching. We can acknowledge the absence of the biblical witness of lament in our ecclesiology and seek to redress that deficiency with worship that more intentionally integrates lament.

Can we change how we approach the problem of injustice in the world? Instead of seeing the problems of the world as laboratories where we apply our know-how and problem-solving skills, we first seek to understand the fullness of the story of suffering. We listen before we diagnose and seek to fix.

Can we begin to more intentionally embody a connection to suffering in the world? We should begin to embrace those who lament. We may find that our flourishing may depend on the lives of those whom we have seen as problems to be fixed rather than as humanity to be embraced. Can our triumphalistic and exceptionalistic assumptions about the rightness of our theology of celebration be tempered by the humility of those who fight for survival under the theology of suffering? We must begin to recognize that the fullness of life that God has in store for us requires the intersection of suffering with celebration.

Dietrich Bonhoeffer serves as an example of an individual steeped in triumphalism and exceptionalism whose life took a different direction under God's sovereign hand. After defeat in World War I, many Germans chafed under the rule of the Weimar Republic. The emergence of the oppressive and genocidal Nazi regime is due in part to the dissatisfaction with the Weimar Republic, which was seen as a weak expression that undermined the self-perception of German exceptionalism. Nazi Germany exploited the deep desire for German exceptionalism.

At first glance, Dietrich Bonhoeffer is an unlikely candidate to resist the Nazi mindset. How did Bonhoeffer move beyond the social-historical context of a German consciousness that elevated German national identity? As a German intellectual, Bonhoeffer would not have escaped the powerful reality of the German nationalistic and imperialistic impulse.

His family background and formation was steeped in German exceptionalism. Bonhoeffer was raised in an intellectual and affluent family: "The upper middle-class Bonhoeffer household employed five servants, and was later joined by a chauffeur."[2] His family of origin reflected a German aristocratic heritage. Karl Von Hase (Bonhoeffer's maternal grandfather) was an "honorary professor in the theology faculty of the University of Breslau. His wife Clara, who had been born Countess Kalkreuth, made her home a meeting-place for scholars and artists."[3] Bonhoeffer's father was a renowned psychiatrist on the faculty of the University of Berlin. Bonhoeffer expressed a pride in his family's good standing in German society: "I am proud to belong to a family that has rendered outstanding service to the German people and nation for generations."[4]

A fierce German nationalism was not excluded from Bonhoeffer's early formation. During World War I, "eight-year-old Dietrich followed the early successes of the German troops with childish patriotism."[5] And "like most Germans, Dietrich at 13 was angered by Article 231 of the Treaty of Versailles, which he could still recite from memory years later."[6] As Geffrey Kelly and Burton Nelson summarize, "Solidarity with the innocent victims of racial hatred and with the multitudes of suffering strewn in the mass graves and rubble of a world war became a passion with Bonhoeffer. Yet the sparks of that passion are barely detectable in his earliest years spent in an atmosphere of relative affluence. He came from a family that enjoyed abundance, even privilege."[7] The sense of exceptionalism and privilege is evident in both the early life story of Bonhoeffer and in the self-perception of Israel toward the exceptional status of their capital city in Lamentations 2:6-9.

Bonhoeffer's family and early life trajectory pointed toward a disengagement with suffering and an immersion in the triumphalistic narrative of early twentieth-century Germany. However, a series of significant events challenged Bonhoeffer's immersion in a celebration context and directed him toward an encounter with suffering and the concomitant theology of suffering. While numerous factors could be considered, I take note of his trans-Atlantic travels, particularly his time at Union Theological Seminary in New York City, where he encountered the Harlem Renaissance and the black church through his experience at Abyssinian Baptist Church. Through his experience at Abyssinian, Bonhoeffer faced challenges to his triumphalistic and nationalistic German worldview. "This year at Union would have an impact beyond the courses he followed. Trying to explain what had happened to him to alter his outlook, in two memorable letters Bonhoeffer says simply that he had become a Christian."[8] His faith moved from the abstract to the real.

In 1931, he arrived in New York to begin a Sloane Graduate Fellowship at Union Theological Seminary. He had been shaped by German theology and high German culture, so he expected to teach and not necessarily to learn. Facing the reality of the onset of the Great Depression, Bonhoeffer offered the theology of Martin Luther inflected with a German accent. The students at Union rejected this abstract intellectualism of theology. Both teacher and students were frustrated by this disconnect. Students scoffed at him, while he ridiculed his students.

However, over the course of his time at Union, Bonhoeffer began to encounter a different worldview. One key influence stemmed from the intersection of his deeply rooted German triumphalism with his experience in an African American church in Harlem. Frank Fisher, the only African American student at Union Seminary, befriended Bonhoeffer and introduced him to Abyssinian Baptist Church.

It was Frank Fisher who made these experiences possible for Bonhoeffer, and they were among the most important of his year in America, perhaps the most important of all to him. Almost every Sunday, and also during the week, he could be found at Abyssinian Baptist Church on West 138th Street in Harlem, where he taught a Sunday school class.[9]

In attending Abyssinian, Bonhoeffer submitted to the authority of the black church and their pastor. The pastor of Abyssinian Church, Adam Clayton Powell, may have introduced two key phrases employed by Bonhoeffer. "'Cheap grace' and 'world come of age' are only two phrases Clayton Powell coins during his long life, 1865-1953, that Dietrich Bonhoeffer (1906-45) uses in his post-Harlem works."[10]

Historian Ralph Clingan posits that the teachings of Powell significantly influenced Bonhoeffer's reflection on Christology. "After learning from Powell, he calls others to work against cheap grace in a world come of age because they love Jesus, phrases he hears Powell use."[11] Bonhoeffer witnessed the life of Christ embodied in the person of Powell. Powell spoke "to move people to do the Gospel. [Powell is not] an individualist, rather he allows the Spirit of the Bible to interpret him, his community and the world as an interrelated whole."[12] The example of Powell provided inspiration for Bonhoeffer, but more so, the community experience of Abyssinian stretched Bonhoeffer's theological imagination.[13]

Most of Bonhoeffer's experiences to this point had been in the context of German exceptionalism and triumphalism. His experience of dealing with suffering would have been the expression of frustration and angst of post–World War I Germany. The triumphalistic German ethos of the twentieth century did not have the ability to deal with suffering. Triumphalism sought to restore Germany's earthly power rather than address the needs of the suffering.

Bonhoeffer's experiences in the United States provided balance to his worldview. The German theological approach of an abstracted faith was challenged by a lived expression of faith; Abyssinian provided an example of an embodied Christology and ecclesiology.

Bonhoeffer observed closely models of Christian lives capable of bridging the gap between spontaneous individual action and the needs of disciplined community life. His friends at Union Seminary and in the black Baptist community provided such paradigms of balance between faith and action and between the individual and the group.[14]

Bonhoeffer encountered the expression of the Harlem Renaissance in its theological and ecclesial expression through Adam Clayton Powell and Abyssinian Baptist Church. He also encountered the writings and the poetry of the Harlem Renaissance. Exposure to these African American writers revealed how much of Bonhoeffer's Christianity was rooted in white, Western, German Christianity. Bonhoeffer was challenged to move beyond the German exceptionalism prevalent during his time. Bonhoeffer's example offers a counternarrative to the triumphalistic exceptionalism and pride that characterized Jerusalem's self-perception prior to her fall. Lamentations challenges God's people to consider an alternative to exceptionalism. It offers the humility of lament.

We must seek to be the church that integrates the theology of suffering with the theology of celebration. We must seek to be the church that engages in both praise and lament. We must seek to be the church that embodies the full narrative of Christ in his suffering and in his triumph. Lamentations offers us a glimpse of what we must seek.

FERGUSON

Midday on August 9, 2014, Michael Brown, an eighteen-year-old African American man, was gunned down by police officer Darren Wilson outside an apartment complex in the St. Louis suburb of Ferguson, Missouri. Accounts vary, but an encounter between a white police officer and a black youth resulted in the death and desecration of a black body and the ignition of a national debate on the worth of black bodies to American society.

The deceased body of Michael Brown was left uncovered out in the heat of an August afternoon for four and a half hours, with friends and family denied access to the body. Michael Brown was deemed no better than roadkill. The body was eventually carted away in the trunk of an SUV and not in an ambulance. These events sparked protests by the community in the St. Louis area asserting that *black lives matter.*

The tragedy of the death of an unarmed black youth was compounded by the lack of an indictment by a grand jury. The decision by the grand jury led to a new round of protests in Ferguson but also ignited a discussion on race relations in the United States. Over the last two months of 2014, on the heels of two nonindictments in the slaying of black men, our nation focused its attention on the drastic inconsistencies inherent in our judicial system. To many observers, black lives had less standing in our nation than white lives.

Rodney King, Trayvon Martin, Mike Brown, Eric Garner and Tamir Rice are part of a long list of black victims of violence. They are victims of an American narrative that devalues black souls, black lives, black bodies and black minds. In response to these tragic events, particularly since the nonindictment of the police officers that murdered Michael Brown and Eric Garner, many evangelicals have been calling for a biblical practice that is often absent in American Christianity—the call to lament.

On one level I am thrilled that evangelicals are discovering the importance of lament in dealing with racial injustice. However, I am concerned that the way lament is being used by some white evangelicals is a watered-down, weak lament that is no lament at all.

Lament is not simply feeling bad that Mike Brown won't be able to go to college. Lament is not simply feeling sad that Eric Garner's kids no longer have a father. Lament is not asserting your right to confront the police because as a white person you won't be treated in the same way that a black protestor may be treated. Lament is not the passive acceptance of tragedy. Lament is not weakly assenting to the status quo. Lament is not simply the expression of sorrow in order to assuage feelings of guilt and the burden of responsibility.

Lamentations responds to a very real tragedy in the history of Israel. What the book of Lamentations teaches about the lost practice of lament will be applied in this epilogue to the racialized events surrounding Ferguson and the ensuing conflict.

DEAD BODIES

Lamentations 1 depicts the reality of death and suffering that leads to the appropriate response of lament. The city of Jerusalem has died, and Lamentations 1 initiates a funeral dirge in response. On both the individual level and on the corporate level, Lamentations 1 challenges us with the necessity of a funeral dirge in the narrative of Ferguson.

The dead body of Michael Brown was not accorded proper respect. The literal dead body lying on the streets of a quiet apartment complex in a Midwestern suburban town demanded a proper funeral dirge in the community. The absence of a funeral dirge creates an emotional and spiritual vacuum. Not only is proper mourning required for the loss of one made in the image of God, but there is the ensuing shame that a human life was handled without dignity.

The use of the funeral-dirge genre in Lamentations reminds us that historical reality cannot be ignored. Funerals are required when we do not deal with the dead bodies of history. Ferguson is a suburb of St. Louis, Missouri, a state that entered the Union as a compromise to ensure the continuation of slavery in the United States. St. Louis was also the site of a significant decision that declared that black lives do not matter. The Dred Scott decision handed down from the federal courthouse in St. Louis denied US citizenship and effectively denied human identity for African Americans.

These historical realities find expression in the complicated narrative of injustice endemic to the Ferguson shooting. The lack of concern for black lives was revealed to be a systemic problem in Ferguson. An investigation of the Ferguson Police Department by the Department of Justice revealed that there was a pattern of unconstitutional policing shaped by a focus on revenue rather than by public safety needs. Ferguson police operated with clear racial disparities that adversely impacted African Americans and showed discriminatory intent.[1] The use of African Americans as a source of revenue reflects a longer history of using black bodies for economic gain.

The declaration that "black lives matter" found expression in an area of our country that had declared that black lives do not matter. We cannot "solve" the problem of race in America while ignoring our deep and painful history. Our tendency to ignore our tainted history may arise from a warped self-perception. We do not need to deal with our tainted past because we have risen above that problematic history and moved to a postracial, colorblind America. An assumed exceptionalism belies the belief that we do not have to deal with our history because through our exceptional status we have overcome the past. The destruction of black bodies and black minds can be justified because their sacrifice helped to build our exceptional nation. Privilege and exceptionalism exempt us from engaging in the necessary work of dealing with our lamentable history.

ALL THE VOICES

As Lamentations moves forward, we encounter a myriad of voices, but the voice of the suffering is often presented as a feminine voice: Jerusalem personified as a woman, the shame of an abused woman, the anguished cry of widows and the suffering endured by mothers. As privileged celebrants, we often have the luxury of ignoring the suffering other, but Lamentations expressed as a feminine voice reminds us to hear the voices of those in our society who often bear the greatest burden of suffering.

As is often the case in the tragic killing of a young black male, the mothers of the slain are often ignored while the voice of the victimizer emerges front and center. The names of Michael Brown's mother and grandmother have faded from memory, but the argument of Darren Wilson's innocence continues. In December 2014 when I visited Ferguson with a group of Christian leaders from all over the country, I was struck by the depth of pain expressed by the older African American women who were present. They voiced a lament that only comes from identifying with others who have had to bury their children.

An important theme that emerged from the frustration over the nonindictments was the call by many to hear the stories of African American brothers and sisters. Instead of being quick to judge, many Christians felt the need to listen. I would strongly affirm that call as an important aspect of lament. We did not need to hear from the ministry experts who pontificated from the comfort of upper-middle-class, white, suburban churches. Instead, the voices of black women who lost their children and the victims of police brutality needed to be the central voices we heard as an important aspect of the practice of lament. Listening to the suffering community does not imply that one party is completely innocent while the other party is completely guilty. Instead, it acknowledges that the dead body in the street is once again the body of a black male. We make special effort, therefore, to listen to the voices of those who have been damaged (and often times retraumatized) by these tragic events.

Lament, however, does not mean silence. In Lamentations 3, we encounter an intensified acrostic that attempts to cover the full expression of human suffering from A to Z. Our lament, therefore, should hear from the full range of voices. At the same time, Lamentations 3 evokes the voice of the narrator (Jeremiah) to speak on behalf of the people. Listening to the previously silenced voices is an essential first step in the practice of lament. But a passive lament that fails to confront injustice fails to consider the power of prophetic advocacy in lament. Many white evangelicals feel helpless when the issue of race comes up. I often hear the refrain from white evangelicals in the midst of a situation like Ferguson, "I don't know what to do!" Many have taken the important first step of being attentive to the long-hidden history of oppression and the personal lament of individuals who have experienced racial injustice. However, Lamentations shifts from a personal lament to a corporate lament with Jeremiah as the prophet-narrator speaking in solidarity with the suffering.

RECAPITULATION

In Lamentations 4 there is a reprisal of the form of the funeral dirge of Lamentations 1 and 2 as well as a recapitulation of the major themes in the first three chapters. Even as voice is given to the formerly silenced voices, we are reminded that the suffering continues. Injustice is not so easily defeated.

The gathering of Christian leaders in Ferguson after the non-indictment of Darren Wilson resulted in a significant commitment to continue to pursue racial justice. The group of Christian leaders from all different backgrounds, generations and ethnicities was inspired by the example of young leaders who led the protest movement in Ferguson. We were impressed with the good work of the local churches that sought to be the shalom presence for the city by hosting and serving those involved in the nonviolent protests.

As we were getting ready to wrap up our final session, there was an energetic optimism about the church's potential response to a deep-seated and systemic racism. In the middle of our final session, various phones in the room started to buzz. One of the participants in the room announced that there had been a decision in the Eric Garner murder—another nonindictment. The confident and optimistic air in the room evaporated. We tried to continue the meeting for a few minutes but we could not.

Several of the African American participants had left the room after the decision was announced. One of the youngest participants in the group was an African American man in his twenties. We could hear him crying in the hallway. The meeting adjourned as the entire group went out to comfort the young man. He began to cry out: "They had video. How could they not indict? There was video this time. . . . Why would I want to bring a child into this world? What future would he have?" His lament weighed heavily on all of us. We were reminded that injustice is not easily defeated. That even after multiple laments had been offered, we couldn't just get over it. There was no "manning up" and no happy, idealized multi-racial worship service to run to. Lament was needed once again. We embraced the young man as he lamented. The inner circle of embrace comprised several older African American women who completely surrounded the young man.

Lament will not allow us to revert to the easy answers. There is no triumphalistic and exceptionalistic narrative of the American church that can cover up injustice. There are no easy answers to unabated suffering. Lament continues.

I pray that the events of Ferguson and the ensuing debate about racial injustice will have a positive impact on the American church. We can no longer brush off the longsuffering of others. The church must recover the practice of lament to combat a triumphalistic narrative that hinders the authentic confrontation of injustice in our world. The oft-forgotten book of Lamentations may help to serve as that corrective.

THE PEOPLE PRAY

The following is a post-Ferguson lament for our nation adapted from Lamentations 5 when the people begin to pray for themselves.

> ¹ Remember, Lord, what happened to Michael Brown and Eric Garner;
>
>   look, and see the disgraceful way they treated their bodies.
> ² Our inheritance of the image of God in every human being has been co-opted and denied by others.
> ³ The children of Eric Garner have become fatherless, widowed mothers grieve their dead children.
> ⁴ We must scrap for our basic human rights;
>   our freedom and our liberty has a great price.
> ⁵ Corrupt officers and officials pursue us and are at our heels;
>   we are weary and find no rest.

⁶ We submitted to uncaring government agencies and to big
business to get enough bread.

⁷ Our ancestors sinned the great sin of instituting slavery;
they are no more—but we bear their shame.

⁸ The system of slavery and institutionalized racism ruled
over us,

and there is no one to free us from their hands.

⁹ We get our bread at the risk of our lives
because of the guns on the streets.

¹⁰ Michael Brown's skin is hot as an oven
as his body lay out in the blazing sun.

¹¹ Women have been violated throughout our nation's history;
black women raped by white slave owners on the plantations.

¹² Noble black men have been hung, lynched and gunned down;
elders and spokesmen are shown no respect.

¹³ Young men can't find work because of unjustly applied laws;
boys stagger under the expectation that their lives are
destined for jail.

¹⁴ The elder statesmen and civil rights leaders are gone from
the city gate;

young people who speak out their protest through music
are silenced.

¹⁵ Trust in our ultimate triumph has diminished;
our triumphant dance has turned to a funeral dirge.

¹⁶ Our sense of exceptionalism has been exposed.
Woe to us, for we have sinned!

¹⁷ Because of this our hearts are faint,
because of these things our eyes grow dim

¹⁸ for our cities lie desolate
with predatory lenders and real estate speculators
prowling over them.

[19] You, Lord, reign forever;
    your throne endures from generation to generation.
[20] Why do you always forget us?
    Why do you forsake us so long?
[21] Restore us to yourself, Lord, that we may return;
    renew our days as of old
[22] unless you have utterly rejected us
    and are angry with us beyond measure.

ACKNOWLEDGMENTS

Thanks to the numerous editors that contributed to the final product: Paul Louis Metzger, Karl Kutz, Daniel Somboonsiri, Al Hsu, Dave Zimmerman and Elissa Schauer. This project would not have been possible without the strong input and patience of InterVarsity Press and the Resonate editors.

Thanks to the faculty and staff of North Park Theological Seminary and University for their ongoing support of my work. In particular, thanks to the dean of North Park Theological Seminary, Dave Kersten; my current academic dean, Stephen Chester; and my former academic dean, Linda Cannell, who helped launch my studies at Duke Divinity School where this project was birthed. My TAs during this project, Evelmyn Ivens, Nilwona Nowlin, Brandon Wrencher and Tim Rhee, provided invaluable help during the process of writing this book.

Thanks to Willie Jennings, Emmanuel Katongole, Kate Bowler, J. Kameron Carter, Grant Wacker, Sam Wells, Mark Chaves, Randy Maddox and Ellen Davis for their inspiration and challenge during my time at Duke Divinity School.

Thanks to Jim Wallis, Rich Stearns, John Perkins, Wayne Gordon and Noel Castellanos, who have graciously allowed me to serve on their respective boards. Their ministries, Sojourners, World Vision and the Christian Community Development Association, offered great encouragement for this work. Thanks in particular to the members of the Theology Committee of the CCDA, including Chris Jehle, Chanequa Walker-Barnes, Danny Carroll, Vince Bantu and Dominique Gilliard. Thanks to Catalyst and Evangelicals for Justice—both communities offered an important source of support and challenge. Thanks to those who have been a part of these two networks over the years: Peter Cha, Greg Yee, Nancy Sugikawa, Jonathan Wu, Andrea Smith, Lisa Sharon Harper, Mae Cannon, Troy Jackson, Sandra Van Opstal, Dan Fan, Emily Price, Randy Woodley, Mark Charles and many others. While he is no longer with us, Richard Twiss remains a powerful influence on my life and ministry. I am thankful for the many different places of connection and shared ministry that I enjoyed with Richard. My friend and mentor Steve Hayner also passed during the writing of this book. I am indebted to the encouragement Steve offered on this project. Elizabeth Pierre, Gary Vanderpol, Larry Kim, and Mark and Valerie Tao have also been a source of support as members of our various church communities over the years.

Most significantly, I live with a profound sense of gratitude for God's provision of my family: to my sisters and their families as they consistently encircle our family with great love; to my mom, whose example continues to deeply shape my spiritual life; to our children, who continue to delight us at every turn; and to my wife, without whom this work would not have been possible. May I be as strong an advocate for you as you have been for me.

Notes

◆

Introduction: A Call to Lament

[1]Randy Woodley, *Shalom and the Community of Creation* (Grand Rapids: Eerdmans, 2012), p. 10.

[2]Walter Brueggemann, *Peace* (St. Louis: Chalice Press, 2001), pp. 3-4.

[3]See Claus Westermann, *Praise and Lament in the Psalms* (Atlanta: John Knox Press, 1981), p. 152.

[4]Denise Hopkins, *Journey Through the Psalms* (St. Louis: Chalice Press, 2002), pp. 5-6. See also Lester Meyer, "A Lack of Laments in the Church's Use of the Psalter," *Lutheran Quarterly* (Spring 1993): 67-78.

[5]Glenn Pemberton, *Hurting with God: Learning to Lament with the Psalms* (Abilene, TX: Abilene Christian University Press, 2012), Kindle loc. 441-45.

[6]Brueggemann, *Peace*, pp. 26-28.

[7]Ibid., pp. 28-29; italics original.

[8]Walter Brueggemann, *The Psalms and the Life of Faith*, ed. Patrick Miller (Minneapolis: Fortress, 1995), p. 102.

[9]Adele Berlin, *Lamentations* (Louisville: Westminster John Knox, 2004), p. 1.

Lamentations 1

[1]In this book I use the tetragrammaton as God's name. The tetragrammaton is the four Hebrew consonants (represented in English as YHWH) of the Hebrew word *Yahweh*, the personal name of God as revealed to Moses in Exodus 3:14. Out of reverence, Jews do not speak this name.

Chapter 1: The Reality of Suffering and Death

[1]Delbert Hillers, *Lamentations: A New Translation with Introduction and Commentary*, Anchor Yale Bible Commentaries (Garden City, NY: Doubleday, 1972), p. 18.

[2]Adele Berlin, *Lamentations* (Louisville: Westminster John Knox, 2004), p. 49.

[3]John Bright, *A History of Israel*, 3rd ed. (Philadelphia: Westminster Press, 1972), p. 331.

[4]This optimism was found in the larger context of pre–World War I American culture. See Barbara Ehrenreich, *Bright-Sided* (New York: Metropolitan Books, 2009), and Kate Bowler, *Blessed* (New York: Oxford, 2013), pp. 12-15, for further reflection on the intersection between American cultural optimism and the church.

[5]George Marsden, *Understanding Fundamentalism and Evangelicalism* (Grand Rapids: Eerdmans, 1991), p. 31. Marsden reveals that this was "an era in which American evangelicalism was so influential that it was virtually a religious establishment," p. 6.

[6]Although a later work, Harvey Cox's *Secular City* reflects the optimism of the Protestant liberal church. Cox envisions the secular city as the pinnacle of human existence. "Secularization designates the content of man's coming of age, urbanization describes the context in which it is occurring. . . . The urban center is the place of human control, of rational planning." Harvey Cox, *Secular City* (New York: Macmillan, 1966), p. 4.

[7]Randall Balmer, *The Making of Evangelicalism* (Waco: Baylor University Press, 2010), p. 33.

[8]Ibid., p. 36.

[9]David Moberg, *The Great Reversal* (New York: J.B. Lippincott, 1972), pp. 25-26.

[10]George Marsden, *Fundamentalism and American Culture* (New York: Oxford, 2006), p. 86.

[11]Ibid., p. 4.

[12]J. A. Thompson, *The Book of Jeremiah*, The New International Commentary on the Old Testament (Grand Rapids: Eerdmans, 1980), p. 547.

[13]D. E. Aune, "Divination," in the *International Standard Biblical Encyclopedia, Vol. 2*, ed. Geoffrey W. Bromiley (Grand Rapids: Eerdmans, 1979), p. 972.

[14]Peter Steinke, *A Door Set Open: Grounding Change in Mission and Hope* (Herndon, VA: The Alban Institute, 2010), Kindle loc. 716-19.

[15]Ehrenreich, *Bright-Sided*, p. 137.

[16]Soong-Chan Rah, *The Next Evangelicalism: Freeing the Church from Western Cultural Captivity* (Downers Grove, IL: InterVarsity Press, 2009), Kindle loc. 518-21.

[17]Ehrenreich, *Bright-Sided*, p. 142.

[18]Shayne Lee and Phillip Luke Sinitiere, *Holy Mavericks* (New York: New York University Press, 2009), Kindle loc. 110-12.

[19]Ehrenreich, *Bright-Sided*, p. 137.

CHAPTER 2: THE FUNERAL DIRGE

[1]Claus Westermann, *Praise and Lament in the Psalms* (Atlanta: John Knox Press, 1981), p. 168.

[2]Eva Harasta and Brian Brock, eds., *Evoking Lament* (New York: T&T Clark, 2009), p. 1.

[3]Sally A. Brown and Patrick D. Miller, eds., *Lament: Reclaiming Practices in Pulpit, Pew, and Public Square* (Louisville: Westminster John Knox, 2005), p. xv.

[4]Kathleen O'Connor, *Lamentations and the Tears of the World* (Maryknoll: Orbis Books, 2002), pp. 19-20.

[5]Kathleen O'Connor, "The Book of Lamentations," *The New Interpreter's Bible* (Nashville: Abingdon, 2001), pp. 1019-20.

[6]S. K. Soderlund, "Lamentations," in *The International Standard Bible Encyclopedia, Volume 3 (K-P)*, ed. Geoffrey W. Bromiley (Grand Rapids: Eerdmans, 1986), p. 67.

[7]Adele Berlin, *Lamentations* (Louisville: Westminster John Knox, 2004), p. 24.

[8]See Mae Elise Cannon, Lisa Sharon Harper, Troy Jackson and Soong-Chan Rah,

Forgive Us: Confessions of a Compromised Faith (Grand Rapids: Zondervan, 2014), p. 13. Quoted from Ibrahim Abdul-Matin, *Green Deen: What Islam Teaches About Protecting the Planet,* book reading at Hue-Man Bookstore, November 12, 2010.

[9]See Albert Raboteau, *Slave Religion: The "Invisible Institution" in the Antebellum South* (New York: Oxford University Press, 1978).

[10]Willie Jennings, *The Christian Imagination: Theology and the Origins of Race* (New Haven & London: Yale University Press, 2010), p. 15.

[11]Ibid., p. 180.

[12]Ibid., p. 178.

[13]Marla F. Frederick, *Between Sundays: Black Women and Everyday Struggles of Faith* (Oakland: University of California Press, 2003), p. 187.

CHAPTER 3: SILENCED VOICES OF SHAME

[1]Norman Gottwald, *Studies in the Book of Lamentations* (London: SCM Press, 1954), p. 62.

[2]Ibid.

[3]Kathleen O'Connor, *Lamentations and the Tears of the World* (Maryknoll: Orbis Books, 2002), p. 17.

[4]Gottwald, *Studies,* p. 62.

[5]Knut M. Heim, "The Personification of Jerusalem and the Drama of Her Bereavement in Lamentations," in *Zion, City of Our God,* ed. Richard S. Hess and Gordon J. Wenham (Grand Rapids: Eerdmans, 1999), p. 141.

[6]Ibid.

[7]Delbert Hillers, *Lamentations: A New Translation with Introduction and Commentary,* Anchor Yale Bible Commentaries (Garden City, NY: Doubleday, 1972), p. 9.

[8]O'Connor, *Lamentations and the Tears of the World,* p. 22.

[9]Adele Berlin, *Lamentations* (Louisville: Westminster John Knox, 2004), p. 53.

[10]Hillers, *Lamentations,* pp. 23-24.

[11]O'Connor, *Lamentations and the Tears of the World,* p. 27.

[12]Andrew Sung Park, "Theology of Pain (the Abyss of Pain)," in *Quarterly Review,* Spring 1989, p. 48.

[13]Young-Hak Hyun, "Minjung the Suffering Servant and Hope," unpublished paper presented at Union Theological Seminary in New York, April 13, 1982. Quoted in Andrew Park, *Racial Conflict and Healing* (New York: Orbis Books, 1996), p. 9.

[14]Park, "Theology of Pain," p. 48.

[15]Ibid., p. 59.

[16]Brené Brown, "Listening to Shame," TED Talk, www.youtube.com/watch?v=psN1DORYYVo.

[17]Emmanuel M. Katongole, *Mirror to the Church: Resurrecting Faith After Genocide in Rwanda* (Grand Rapids: Zondervan, 2009), Kindle loc. 77.

[18]O'Connor, *Lamentations and the Tears of the World,* p. 14.

[19]Ibid., p. 28.

[20]See www.redletterchristians.org. Accessed on June 9, 2013.

[21]See www.qideas.org. Accessed on June 9, 2013.

[22]Claus Westermann, *Praise and Lament in the Psalms* (Atlanta: John Knox Press, 1981), p. 155.

[23]Ibid., p. 213.

[24]Walter Brueggemann, *Psalms and the Life of Faith* (Minneapolis: Fortress Press, 1995), Kindle loc. 1151, 1158.

[25]Xuan Huong Thi Pham, *Mourning in the Ancient Near East and the Hebrew Bible* (Sheffield, England: Sheffield Academic Press, 1999), p. 190.

[26]Katongole, *Mirror to the Church*, Kindle loc. 1596.

CHAPTER 4: GOD IS FAITHFUL

[1]Leslie C. Allen, *A Liturgy of Grief* (Grand Rapids: Baker Academic, 2011), Kindle loc. 1256-58.

[2]J. Richard Middleton and Brian J. Walsh, *Truth Is Stranger Than It Used to Be* (Downers Grove, IL: InterVarsity Press, 1995), p. 44.

[3]See Soong-Chan Rah, *The Next Evangelicalism* (Downers Grove, IL: InterVarsity Press, 2009).

[4]"In the year 1900, Europe and North America comprised 82 percent of the world's Christian population. In 2005, European and North American comprised 39 percent of the world Christian population." Ibid., Kindle loc. 68-70.

CHAPTER 5: LAMENT OVER A CITY

[1]Kathleen O'Connor, "The Book of Lamentations," in *The New Interpreter's Bible* (Nashville: Abingdon, 2001), p. 1019.

[2]S. N. Kramer, trans., "Lamentation over the Destruction of Ur" and "Lamentation over the Destruction of Sumer and Ur," in *Ancient Near Eastern Texts Relating to the Old Testament*, 3rd ed., ed. James B. Pritchard (Princeton: Princeton University, 1969), pp. 455-63, 611-19.

[3]F. W. Dobbs-Allsopp, *Lamentations* (Louisville: John Knox Press, 2002), p. 9.

[4]Ibid. See also F. W. Dobbs-Allsopp, *Weep, O Daughter of Zion: A Study of the City-Lament Genre in the Hebrew Bible* (Rome: Biblical Institute Press, 1993).

[5]Mark Biddle notes that "the goddess in the city-laments functions as Jerusalem does in the book of Lamentations." Biddle, "The Figure of Lady Jerusalem," in *The Canon in Comparative Perspective,* Scripture in Context IV (Lewiston, NY: Mellen Press, 1991), p. 182.

[6]Dobbs-Allsopp, *Lamentations*, p. 79.

[7]Ibid., p. 7.

[8]Ibid., p. 9.

[9]Ibid., p. 12.

[10]For example, to the Greeks, "the *polis* (city) meant far more . . . than a place on the

map; it meant the place where people achieve unity." Richard Sennett, *Flesh and Stone: The Body and the City in Western Civilization* (New York: W. W. Norton, 1994), p. 39. The *polis* serves as both the concrete concept of a political entity and also the abstract concept for collective human life and a social-political entity.

[11] As Augustine writes, "The earthly city was created by self-love reaching the point of contempt for God, the Heavenly City by the love of God carried as far as contempt of self. In fact, the earthly city glories in itself, the Heavenly City glories in the Lord. The former looks for glory from men, the latter finds its highest glory in God." Augustine, *City of God*, trans. Henry Bettenson (New York: Penguin, 1972), p. 593.

[12] Winthrop S. Hudson, *Religion in America,* 3rd ed. (New York: Charles Scribner's Sons, 1981), pp. 20-21.

[13] William A. Clebsch, *From Sacred to Profane America* (New York: Harper & Row, 1968), p. 39. Harvie Conn also notes that the colonial Puritan hoped that "New England would one day become the New Jerusalem." Harvie M. Conn, *The American City and the Evangelical Church* (Grand Rapids: Baker Books, 1994), p. 28.

[14] Robert Orsi, *Gods of the City* (Bloomington: Indiana University Press, 1999), p. 6.

[15] Amanda I. Seligman, *Block by Block: Neighborhoods and Public Policy on Chicago's West Side* (Chicago: University of Chicago Press, 2005), pp. 210-11.

[16] Isabel Wilkerson, *The Warmth of Other Suns* (New York: Vintage, 2010), p. 378.

[17] Churches in the suburbs exhibited significant numerical growth in the latter half of the twentieth century. Winthrop Hudson notes that while $26 million was spent on new church buildings in 1945, that number steadily increased to over $1 billion by 1960 (Hudson, *Religion in America*, p. 384n45). Harvie Conn asserts that these numbers reflect the expansion of churches in the suburbs requiring new buildings (Conn, *The American City and the Evangelical Church*, p. 97). While church attendance increased in the suburbs, Herbert Gans's 1967 research on a quintessential suburban town revealed that families that move from the city to suburbia entailed no change in church or synagogue attendance (Herbert Gans, *The Levittowners: Ways of Life and Politics in a New Suburban Community* [New York: Columbia University Press, 1967], p. 264). The move to the suburbs did not yield a high rate of conversion that led to increased church attendance. Instead, suburban church growth relied on the population shift of the white community from urban centers to suburban outposts.

Chapter 6: Privilege and Exceptionalism

[1] Norman Gottwald, *Studies in the Book of Lamentations* (London: SCM Press, 1954), p. 19.

[2] Adele Berlin, *Lamentations* (Louisville: Westminster John Knox, 2004), p. 1.

[3] Ibid., p. 67.

[4] Walter Brueggemann in the foreword to James E. Atwood's *America and Its Guns: A Theological Expose* (Eugene, OR: Wipf and Stock, 2012), pp. xi-xii.

CHAPTER 7: ALL OF THE VOICES ARE HEARD

[1]Kathleen O'Connor, *Lamentations and the Tears of the World* (Maryknoll: Orbis Books, 2002), p. 83.

[2]Adele Berlin, *Lamentations* (Louisville: Westminster John Knox, 2004), p. 13.

[3]Knut M. Heim, "The Personification of Jerusalem and the Drama of Her Bereavement in Lamentations," in *Zion, City of Our God,* ed. Richard S. Hess and Gordon J. Wenham (Grand Rapids: Eerdmans, 1999), p. 142.

[4]F. W. Dobbs-Allsopp, *Lamentations* (Louisville: John Knox Press, 2002), p. 41.

[5]Berlin, *Lamentations,* p. 13.

[6]Clement Gayle, *George Liele: Pioneer Missionary to Jamaica* (Kingston, Jamaica: Jamaica Baptist Union, 1982), p. 3.

[7]Edward A. Holmes, "George Liele: Negro Slavery's Prophet of Deliverance," *Baptist Quarterly* 20 (October 1964): 345.

[8]Ibid., p. 346.

[9]Gayle, *George Liele,* p. 17, and John Clarke, *The Voice of Jubilee: A Narrative of the Baptist Mission, Jamaica from Its Commencement* (London: J. Snow, 1865), p. 32.

[10]Randy Woodley, *Shalom and the Community of Creation* (Grand Rapids: Eerdmans, 2012), pp. 10, 21.

[11]O'Connor, *Lamentations and the Tears of the World,* p. 9.

[12]Ibid.

[13]Emmanuel Katongole, *The Sacrifice of Africa: A Political Theology for Africa* (Grand Rapids: Eerdmans, 2011), p. 195.

CHAPTER 8: A STRUCTURE FOR LAMENT

[1]Kathleen O'Connor, "The Book of Lamentations," *The New Interpreter's Bible* (Nashville: Abingdon, 2001), p. 1018.

[2]Norman Gottwald, *Studies in the Book of Lamentations* (London: SCM Press, 1954), p. 29.

[3]Delbert Hillers, *Lamentations: A New Translation with Introduction and Commentary,* Anchor Yale Bible Commentaries (Garden City, NY: Doubleday, 1972), p. xxvii.

[4]Ibid., p. 139.

[5]Gottwald, *Studies in the Book of Lamentations,* p. 30.

[6]Ibid., p. 28.

[7]F. W. Dobbs-Allsopp, *Lamentations* (Louisville: John Knox Press, 2002), p. 18.

[8]Jenny Berrien, Omar McRoberts and Christopher Winship, "Religion and the Boston Miracle: The Effect of Black Ministry on Youth Violence," in *Who Will Provide? The Changing Role of Religion in American Social Welfare,* ed. Mary Jo Bane and Brent Coffin (Boulder, CO: Westview Press, 2000), p. 267.

CHAPTER 9: ALL OF IT IS PERSONAL

[1]Claus Westermann, *Praise and Lament in the Psalms* (Atlanta: John Knox Press, 1981), p. 162.

[2]Kathleen O'Connor, *Lamentations and the Tears of the World* (Maryknoll: Orbis Books, 2002), p. 47.

CHAPTER 10: A GLIMMER OF HOPE

[1]Delbert Hillers, *Lamentations: A New Translation with Introduction and Commentary*, Anchor Yale Bible Commentaries (Garden City, NY: Doubleday, 1972), p. 70.

[2]Ibid.

[3]R. Laird Harris, Gleason L. Archer and Bruce K. Waltke, *Theological Wordbook of the Old Testament* (Chicago: Moody Publishers, 2003), p. 841.

[4]Ibid., p. 52.

[5]William L. Holladay, *A Concise Hebrew and Aramaic Lexicon of the Old Testament* (Grand Rapids: Eerdmans, 1988), p. 20.

[6]F. W. Dobbs-Allsopp, *Lamentations* (Louisville: John Knox Press, 2002), p. 119.

[7]Richard Lovelace, *Dynamics of Spiritual Life* (Downers Grove, IL: InterVarsity Press, 1979), p. 75.

[8]Adele Berlin, *Lamentations* (Louisville: Westminster John Knox, 2004), pp. 95-96.

[9]Ibid., p. 95.

[10]Mae Elise Cannon, Lisa Sharon Harper, Troy Jackson and Soong-Chan Rah, *Forgive Us: Confessions of a Compromised Faith* (Grand Rapids: Zondervan, 2014), pp. 205-6.

[11]Rabbi Morris Silverman and Rabbi Hillel E. Silverman, *Tishah B'Av Services*, expanded ed. (Bridgeport, CT: The Prayer Book Press of Media Judaica, 1972), p. i.

[12]Ibid., p. i.

[13]Ibid., p. ii.

[14]Ibid.

CHAPTER 11: PERSISTING IN LAMENT

[1]F. W. Dobbs-Allsopp, *Lamentations* (Louisville: John Knox Press, 2002), pp. 6-12.

[2]Kathleen O'Connor, "The Book of Lamentations," in *The New Interpreter's Bible* (Nashville: Abingdon, 2001), pp. 1019-20.

[3]Kathleen O'Connor, *Lamentations and the Tears of the World* (Maryknoll: Orbis Books, 2002), p. 102.

[4]Nancy Lee, *The Singers of Lamentations* (Boston: Brill Academic, 2002), p. 33.

[5]Sally A. Brown and Patrick D. Miller, eds., *Lament: Reclaiming Practices in Pulpit, Pew, and Public Square* (Louisville: Westminster John Knox, 2005), p. xvi.

[6]O'Connor, *Lamentations and the Tears of the World*, p. 10.

[7]Carleen Mandolfo, *Daughter Zion Talks Back to the Prophets* (Atlanta: Society of Biblical Literature, 2007), p. 76.

[8]Claus Westermann, *Lamentations: Issues and Interpretation* (Minneapolis: Fortress Press, 1994), p. 11.

[9]Nancy Lee asserts that "Lamentations does also show a decided movement from the dirge genre at the outset to the lament genre across the five chapters, though this movement is not simply linear but is an interplay of voices between the two genres while moving to a final sustained communal lament prayer in Lam 5" (Lee, *The Singers of Lamentations*, p. 37).

[10]O'Connor, *Lamentations and the Tears of the World*, p. 59.

[11]Adele Berlin, *Lamentations* (Louisville: Westminster John Knox, 2004), p. 104.

[12]Patrick D. Miller, *Interpreting the Psalms* (Philadelphia: Fortress Press, 1986), p. 11.

[13]Ibid., p. 1.

[14]Ibid., p. 38.

[15]Mya Frazier, "Costly Red Campaign Reaps Meager $18 Million," *Advertising Age*, March 5, 2007, http://adage.com/article/news/costly-red-campaign-reaps-meager -18-million/115287/.

[16]Emmanuel M. Katongole, *Mirror to the Church: Resurrecting Faith After Genocide in Rwanda* (Grand Rapids: Zondervan, 2009), Kindle loc. 84-85.

CHAPTER 12: A BROKEN WORLD

[1]Adele Berlin, *Lamentations* (Louisville: Westminster John Knox, 2004), p. 105.

[2]Kathleen O'Connor, *Lamentations and the Tears of the World* (Maryknoll: Orbis Books, 2002), p. 61.

[3]Delbert Hillers, *Lamentations: A New Translation with Introduction and Commentary*, Anchor Yale Bible Commentaries (Garden City, NY: Doubleday, 1972), p. 80.

[4]Ibid., p. 89.

[5]Lance Lewis, "Black Pastoral Leadership and Church Planting," in *Aliens in the Promised Land*, ed. Anthony Bradley (Phillipsburg, NJ: Presbyterian and Reformed Publishing, 2013), pp. 27-28.

[6]See Zach Hoag, "What Furtick's Millions Might Mean," February 10, 2014, www .patheos.com/blogs/zhoag/2014/02/10/what-furticks-millions-the-we-serve-a -lead-pastor-mantra-might-mean, and Emily Harris, "On God's Stage: Elevation Church," January 2014, www.charlottemagazine.com/Charlotte-Magazine/January -2014/The-Story-of-Elevation-Church.

[7]Vinoth Ramachandra, "Reformed Amnesia," at http://vinothramachandra .wordpress.com/2013/03/28/reformed-amnesia.

[8]F. W. Dobbs-Allsopp, *Lamentations* (Louisville: John Knox Press, 2002), pp. 133-34.

[9]O'Connor, *Lamentations and the Tears of the World*, p. 67.

[10]Berlin, *Lamentations*, p. 112.

[11]Mae Elise Cannon, Lisa Sharon Harper, Troy Jackson and Soong-Chan Rah, *Forgive Us: Confessions of a Compromised Faith* (Grand Rapids: Zondervan, 2014), pp. 21-33.

[12]Berlin, *Lamentations*, p. 113.

[13]Dobbs-Allsopp, *Lamentations*, p. 137.

CHAPTER 13: A LAMENT FOR THEMSELVES

[1]F. W. Dobbs-Allsopp, *Lamentations* (Louisville: John Knox Press, 2002), p. 140. See Psalms 44, 60, 74, 79, 80, 83.

[2]Delbert Hillers, *Lamentations: A New Translation with Introduction and Commentary*, Anchor Yale Bible Commentaries (Garden City, NY: Doubleday, 1972), p. 102.

[3]Leslie C. Allen, *A Liturgy of Grief* (Grand Rapids: Baker Academic, 2011), Kindle loc. 2595-96.

[4]Walter Brueggemann, *The Psalms and the Life of Faith*, ed. Patrick Miller (Minneapolis: Fortress, 1995), Kindle loc. 1177.

[5]Claus Westermann, *Praise and Lament in the Psalms* (Atlanta: John Knox Press, 1981), p. 261.

[6]Brueggemann, *Psalms and the Life of Faith*, Kindle loc. 1177.

[7]Nancy Lee, *The Singers of Lamentations* (Boston: Brill Academic, 2002), p. 35.

[8]Brueggemann, *Psalms and the Life of Faith*, Kindle loc. 1177.

[9]Ibid., Kindle loc. 1188.

[10]Westermann, *Praise and Lament*, p. 261.

[11]Ibid.

[12]Allen, *A Liturgy of Grief*, Kindle loc. 2615-16.

[13]Brueggemann, *Psalms and the Life of Faith*, Kindle loc. 103-4.

[14]Luke Bretherton, *Christianity and Contemporary Politics* (Chichester, UK: Wiley-Blackwell, 2010), p. 213.

[15]Kathleen O'Connor, *Lamentations and the Tears of the World* (Maryknoll: Orbis Books, 2002), p. 73.

[16]Adele Berlin, *Lamentations* (Louisville: Westminster John Knox, 2004), p. 118.

[17]Ibid., p. 120.

[18]"Take My Hand, Precious Lord," written by Rev. Thomas A. Dorsey.

[19]Dobbs-Allsopp, *Lamentations*, p. 141.

[20]Berlin, *Lamentations*, p. 124.

[21]O'Connor, *Lamentations and the Tears of the World*, p. 77.

[22]Berlin, *Lamentations*, p. 125.

[23]Richard Sennett, *Flesh and Stone: The Body and the City in Western Civilization* (New York: W. W. Norton, 1994), p. 374.

[24]Samuel Wells, "Ministry on an Urban Estate," lecture presented at the National Readers' Course, Duke University, Durham, NC, August 2001.

CONCLUSION

[1]Samuel Wells, *Improvisation* (Grand Rapids: Brazos Press, 2004), p. 24.

[2]Ferdinand Schlingensiepen, *Dietrich Bonhoeffer 1906-1945: Martyr, Thinker, Man*

of Resistance, trans. Isabel Best (New York: T&T Clark, 2010), p. 3.

[3]Ibid., p. 3.

[4]Ibid., p. 2.

[5]Ibid., p. 11.

[6]Ibid., p. 15.

[7]Geffrey B. Kelly and F. Burton Nelson, "Editor's Introduction," in *A Testament to Freedom: The Essential Writings of Dietrich Bonhoeffer* (New York: HarperCollins, 1990), p. 5.

[8]Geffrey Kelly, "Dietrich Bonhoeffer (1906-1945): A Witness to Christian Faith in the Nazi Era," *Fides et historia* 29, no. 2 (June 1997): 13.

[9]Schlingensiepen, *Dietrich Bonhoeffer,* p. 65.

[10]Ralph Garlin Clingan, *Against Cheap Grace in a World Come of Age* (New York: Peter Lang, 2002), p. ix.

[11]Ibid.

[12]Ibid., p. x.

[13]See also Reggie Williams, *Bonhoeffer's Black Jesus* (Waco, TX: Baylor University Press, 2014).

[14]Ruth Zerner, "Dietrich Bonhoeffer's American Experiences: People, Letters, and Papers from Union Seminary," *The Union Seminary Quarterly Review* 31, no. 4 (1976): 261.

EPILOGUE: FERGUSON

[1]United States Department of Justice Civil Rights Division, "Investigation of the Ferguson Police Department," March 4, 2015, p. 2, www.justice.gov/sites/default /files/opa/press-releases/attachments/2015/03/04/ferguson_police_department _report.pdf.